EYES
OF A
Woman

LESTER WITCHER JR.

Copyright © 2022 Lester Witcher Jr..

All rights reserved. No part of this book may be reproduced, stored, or transmitted by any means—whether auditory, graphic, mechanical, or electronic—without written permission of both publisher and author, except in the case of brief excerpts used in critical articles and reviews. Unauthorized reproduction of any part of this work is illegal and is punishable by law.

ISBN: 979-8-88640-358-9 (sc)
ISBN: 979-8-88640-359-6 (hc)
ISBN: 979-8-88640-360-2 (e)

Because of the dynamic nature of the Internet, any web addresses or links contained in this book may have changed since publication and may no longer be valid. The views expressed in this work are solely those of the author and do not necessarily reflect the views of the publisher, and the publisher hereby disclaims any responsibility for them.

One Galleria Blvd., Suite 1900, Metairie, LA 70001
1-888-421-2397

First and foremost, I would like to thank my Lord and Savior Jesus Christ for blessing me with this amazingly unique talent. And for giving me the strength, courage and determination to produce the follow up to "Eyes of a Man" with "Eyes of a Woman".

This book is dedicated to all of those that are imbedded within this book, from all of my family, extended family, friends, survivors and the angels that we lost. I want to thank all of the folks that made this possible: Judy Witcher, Ruby Brown, Estella Williams, Annie Holt, Margie Harvey, Lester Witcher Sr., Lois Monts Witcher, Darlene Mack, Shirley Lynch, Karin Taylor, Jennifer Hammond, Colleen Blake, Melody & Rossie Ashlock, Dexter Parraway, Jennifer & Dave Fisher, Ann Snyder, Diana Snyder, Dea J.B. Brown, Diane Bruce, Clinton Fields Jr., Twyla Wilson, Bernice Brewer, Debbie Clark, Shanna Clark, Torrey Sutton, Erin O'Brien, Marlene & Liz Bradley, Carolyn Rupp, Viola E. "Vi" Purnell, Hailee Waltz, Andrea & Mark Cimabue, Mr. & Mrs. DeBright, Vickie Stoker, Emmy Kavanagh, Joyce D. Lewis Hunter, Tessa, Daniel Webster Stayathome, Bernadette Stayathome, Audrey & Ray Woods, Gabriella Faith, Maria Rios, Rebecca Ann Taylor, April Hofacker, Sharon Black, Gwen C. DiNicola, Linda Massey, Patricia C. Moore, Anthony Scarbro, The Scarbro Family, William Scott Cowan Jr., Joan Griffith, Sheila Williams, Collin Michael Gilbert, Annamarie "Nancy" Borden, Lori Borden-Ashcraft, Carol Gundle, Teresa Earl, Al, Jackie, Lydia & Ben, Ruth & Kitty, and those that I may have missed I'm truly sorry forgive me, and you know who you are love you!

Last but not least Chapter 1 through 5 and Book Cover photos by David "the master" Heitur for the amazing work he put into making these photos reach the stars. Thank you!

Contents

Chapter 1   First Light 1
   Art of a Poet's Soul 2
   As You Are 3
   Blessing to Me 5
   Blonde Beauty 6
   Born Again 7
   Cloud 9 8
   Daddy's Girl 9
   Damaged Goods 10
   Dangerous 11
   Daughter Forever 12
   Destiny 13
   Feel Used 14
   Finish Last 15
   Frightened 16
   Give Up on You 17
   Godmother 18
   Greatest Gift 20
   Half Crazy 21
   Handsome Specimen 22
   Haunted Past 23
   I am Broken 25
   I Don't Like 26
   I Won't Stand in Your Way 28
   Just Because 29
   Last Breath 30
   Last Kiss 31
   Left Behind 32
   Loving Me 33
   Lust for You 34
   Marry Me 35
   Mouthwatering 36

My Soul is Lost 37
My Soul Will Be Free 38
P.A.T.L. (Precious All Time Love) 39
Precious Gem 40
Saving Grace 41
Sorry! 42
Stranded 43
Sweet Kisses 45
The Next Generation 46
Treasure Chest 47
Twinkle in Her Eye 48

Chapter 2   Angels 49
As Dove's Fly 50
Darling Momma 51
E.R.I.N. (Elegant Royalty In Nature) 52
Family Love 53
Fly Away 54
God Has My Soul 55
God in Heaven 56
Heaven's Love 57
Love Everlasting 58
Mighty Clouds of Joy 59
Mom, Dad & Sis 60
My Spirit Free 61
No One like You 62
Queen of My Heart 63
Rebecca Ann Taylor 64
Remembering You Auntie 65
Remembering You Mom 66
Shining Star 67
Spirit in Heaven 68
Temple of the Lord 69
True Angel 70
Winds of My Sail 71

Chapter 3   Bundles of Joy... 73
    Baby Nova... 74
    Our Sweet Baby Girl... 75
    Wings to Soar in Heaven.. 76
    With All My Heart... 77
    You're My Blessing... 78

Chapter 4   Festivities... 79
    Christmas Prayer to My Daughter................................... 80
    Family Tree Christmas... 81
    Happy 15th Anniversary.. 82
    Happy 39th Valentine's Day Mark.................................... 83
    Happy 40th Anniversary... 84
    Happy Birthday Dad 2019.. 85
    Happy Birthday Vickie.. 86
    Happy Mother's Day Auntie 2019.................................... 87
    Happy Mother's Day Grandmom 2019........................... 88
    Happy Mother's Day Mom 2019..................................... 89
    Happy Mother's Day to all Moms................................... 90
    Happy Valentine's Day Ladylove..................................... 91
    Happy Valentine's Day My Love..................................... 92
    Holiday Love.. 93
    Merry Christmas and Happy New Year.......................... 94
    Blessing to You on Christmas Day................................... 95

Chapter 5   Inspirations... 97
    Annamarie Nancy Borden... 98
    Cast Another Note Commits Energy Revitalization...... 99
    Get Well Soon Debbie!... 100
    Greatest Masterpiece.. 101
    H.A.I.L.E.E... 102
    Heaven's Light.. 103
    Heaven's Warmth 104
    L.E.S.T.E.R. 105

L.I.F.E (Love in Faith Everyday).. 106
Love Joy 107
M.O.M. 108
Mates of the Soul Forever 109
Memories of a Lifetime... 110
My Letter to God 111
My Sister.. 112
Poem to the Parents... 113
Rose 114
Sweet Dot... 115
Victory... 116
World's Greatest Stepson 117

Chapter 6   After Dark.. 119
Black & Sexy 120
Exquisite 121
Head to Toe.. 123
Hug & Kiss 125
I Can't Get Enough of You... 126
Latin Lover.. 128
Long-Distance Love Affair... 130
Oh My! 131
On the Horizon.. 132
One in a Million 134
S. L. (Stimulating Love) 135
Sea Blue Dress.. 136
Spoken Words.. 138

Chapter 7   Memoires.. 141
Eyes of a Woman 142
Last Prayer... 155
Love Beyond Love.. 157
My Boo... 159
No One Else 167

Perfect Crush... 169
Precious Angel... 170
Pretty Smile... 174
Spirit Adrift.. 176
Sweet Gentle Woman... 178
To Love and To Hold... 179
Vibrant Angel... 181
WOW!... 182

Chapter 1

FIRST LIGHT

Art of a Poet's Soul

As I enter my studio to capture my vision on canvas
I open the drapes that look out upon the waterfall
As I pick up my paint brush and use gentle strokes
Because I am lost in love for my sweetheart
All I do day and night is yearn for my baby
As the tingling of your kiss runs through my veins
Just as the blood flows so does my love for you
As each brush stroke expresses, what I feel inside
Because what you hear or see, is the art of a poet's soul

As I walk onto the balcony to listen to the sound of the waterfall
Makes me want to hold you and lock you away in my arms
As the cool breeze blows through the glowing curls in your hair
And the sun shines through your sheer dress upon your skin
As I look into your tender green eyes like I'm in a trance
Because moments like this confirm the love in my heart
That you have implanted inside the core of my spirit
As my love pours out from the art of a poet's soul

As you begin to shiver from the cool breeze outside
You move in close and bury your head into my chest
As I place my robe around you and cuddle you close
You look up at me with a passionate smile on your face
As you balance on your toes to give me a big kiss
And in your soft voice you tell me you love me
Because you think you're the luckiest woman alive
And how I make you feel is nothing you ever faced
Because nothing can compare to the art of a poet's soul

As You Are

Every time I look at you, I fall in love
Because it soothes my soul
I cannot stop my heart from beating fast
As I look deep into your eyes
Because your touch gives me goose bumps
While my body becomes weak inside
As you are the stars in my midnight sky
That brightens my heart and soul
While I look upon the moonlight
As you are

When I am not feeling well
You comfort me from head to toe
And when times seem rough
You make sure that you are there
To hold me close inside your arms
Because you will always be by my side
Even when things seem to be lost
However, you made a promise to me
That no matter what you will be there
Because I love you more each day
As you are

Our souls have been lost for some time
However, when you came into my life
You revived my spirit within
While God provided me with you
Because we were in need of a great blessing
And God brought us together
Because he knew, we needed each other
As when we first met, I felt your heart
When you touched my hand
And it felt so pure in my soul
Because I fell head over heels for you
And from that moment I wanted you in my life
As you are

Blessing to Me

Becky if I look you up in the dictionary it says amazing
Because you can bring sunshine to a cloudy day
As your smile can outshine the lights in a room
Because you are truly thoughtful, kind and loving
And I want to express my deepest appreciation for you
As angels come in many forms to grace our presence
And you're an angel that was assigned to my existence
Because God put blessings in your life for a reason
And you are worth every reason known to man
I pray your kindheartedness engraves my soul
Thank you, Becky, for being a blessing to me

Blonde Beauty

Let me tell you this story about this sexy blonde beauty
I was sitting at my desk at work one day
And she called me on the phone to set up a meeting
As I accepted and she decided to come over to my desk
And I was getting my notes together to talk business
As the time was getting closer to the top of the hour
I didn't have anything on my mind but business
As I was finishing up a report I hear a knock at my desk
And as I turn to see who it could be standing there
It was this gorgeous blonde beauty

As she was standing there in this full RED body dress
That just turned heads as folks walked by her in the aisle
As I began to have shortness of breath captivated by her beauty
Staying focused on the task at hand was a top priority
But as I searched for a chair for her to sit down
And the looks on the faces of my teammates was priceless
Because they thought I was so lucky to be in her presence
And I couldn't shake the befuddled cloud in my mind
Because she had my composure all disorganized inside
But I had to pull it together and stay focused on business
As I gently slide the chair in for her to sit down
And I began to go over my processes with her
As I couldn't even make eye contact as we spoke
Because she is a sexy blonde beauty

Born Again

My mind is working overtime
Because all I can do is, think of you
It keeps playing tricks with my heart
As the hours pass by slowly
Nevertheless, I know
I cannot wait for that moment
Because I will be with my baby again
The journey has been long for us
Because we needed this time apart
With all that we had to endure together
It seems right to give what we had a chance
To feel born again!

As our paths have come full circle to meet again
I always wondered how you were doing without me
Because I knew, I was never the same without you
My life has been spinning out of control away from you
As I couldn't eat and was not sleeping at night
Because you were on my mind every minute
As I tried to keep busy to not go half-crazy
However, that method never succeeded to blossom
Because my soul wanted you more than my heart
As it drove me to the brink of no return
However, when I ran into you in the supermarket
It made me feel born again!

Cloud 9

Sitting here with you across the table from me
Was just so amazingly heart wrenching
Because I almost forgot how beautiful you really are
And I know you noticed I could not look at you
Because if I did it would be a constant stare
And I did not want you to be scared away
Therefore, I am using less eye contact than normal
Nevertheless, you caught on to my nervousness
And you began to crack jokes to loosen me up
As always, your beauty can mesmerize my soul
As you, cause me to be on Cloud 9

As the minutes pass by I got a shiver up my spine
Because I am in so much of a daze from your smile
As it brightened the room and my heart from within
I just fell deep into the words that you were speaking
And I just lost myself in the softness of your voice
Because if you were mine I would treat you like my queen
I know that by me saying this it would give you doubts
However, I would make it a reality if I could have you
As I snap out of my afternoon day dream of you
As you, cause me to be on Cloud 9

I always wondered about what if for us as a couple
And I know that being with you would be an honor
Because if happiness was a picture it would be us
Nevertheless, you and I would be farfetched
Because there would be so much at stake for us
And with all of it, I am willing to risk it all for you
Because I always felt something special for you
As we just never had the opportunity to find out
Now it seems like fate is giving us the chance
Because I can't get you out of the thoughts in my mind
As you, cause me to be on Cloud 9

Daddy's Girl

As I sit here and stare out upon the moonlight
You cross my mind daddy and my love for you
Because I think back to how you protected me
As I grew year after year from a baby to little girl
And then from a little girl to a teenager
As you held me in your arms as I became an adult
Those memorable moments give me Goosebumps
Because as I sit here all alone in deep thought
I know I'm your baby girl and you love me
With every passing minute of the day
You still call me Daddy's Girl

As my tears begin to run down my face in joy
Nothing in this world can change my happiness
Because I cherish every moment we share together
And I soar among the clouds when you're near me
Because when I'm weak you are my strength
When I'm sad you're the glue that holds me tight
And the blessing that soothes my spirit within
Because I'm Daddy's Girl

Damaged Goods

I am on my last day on the seas before I head home
It has been an interesting two months away for me
As I tried to focus on my soul's life struggles
Each day became more intense to overcome the hurdles
That my inner core has surrendered to all this suffering
All of this distress has been overwhelming to me
Just as you try to recover and move forward
All of those woes tend to churn like a stomachache
As it makes me feel like Damaged Goods

As the ship begins to dock from this long journey
I gather my things to prepare to get off the ship
Because my solitude is just about over
As I will go back to my everyday routine
However, I am not feeling any better about myself
Because my internal core has burned out
And I just want to go somewhere and hide forever
Because my soul feels like Damaged Goods

I figured the long trip would do me some good
Because I needed to find my identity again
However, it just brought all the bad to the surface
As I tried to release the unhealthy scars from my soul
And focus on the future events that may come into my life
No matter how much I tried it led me back to sorrow
All I can recommend to anyone that ever feels this way
Try to keep yourself from crumbling deep inside
Because I hate feeling like Damaged Goods

Dangerous

As the birds sing outside of my window pane
And the sun shines bright through the curtains
I roll over to stretch to begin a new day
As I stand to my feet and walk to the window
The melody of the birds' songs soothes my soul
As I open the blinds to feel the fall breeze
And to watch the birds sing in the trees
I realize that I am missing you dearly
And how you have captivated my heart
Just knowing this makes you Dangerous

As the water runs down my back from the shower
And the cool breeze blows through the bathroom window
I still hear the birds singing outside in the trees
And my mind begins to picture your face
As the beautiful sound captures your beauty in my mind
And I begin to see you standing in the shower mist
With your smile brightening up the room
As I reach out to grab your hand into mine
The touch of the water brings me back to earth
And with my heart pounding faster with every beat
Just knowing this makes you Dangerous

Daughter Forever

When I was a little girl you dreamed with me
That I would sprout up one day from a little pea
You gave me lots of hugs and kisses too
Then that day came as I blossomed for you
As I stand next to you with a smile on my face
I pray to the Lord that our lives nurture with grace
Because I love you from within with all my heart
Just as you whisper to me we will never be apart
Years pass us by as we spend time together
But as God knows we are like two birds of a feather
God has blessed me with you forever in my heart
And I am so proud to be your daughter forever!

Destiny

Do you believe in the art of faith?
I do because I had you come into my life
You have brought blissful feelings to my soul
Because my feelings for you run very deep
As we talk it intensifies how I feel
I do not think there is a thing called coincidence
Because I know, things happen for a reason
And God has control over all things in life
Because he has brought us to this crossroad
As we are given the opportunity for Destiny

I ask myself the question of why now?
Because after 20 years I still have feelings for you
And what makes it so crazy they have increased
More now than ever before and we were not an item
Which makes those feelings seep out of my pores
As I can't shake you out of my mind
You know to a point of what you are doing to me
Because you finally have caused me to blush
Not just on the outside but inside my soul
Because these are the feelings of Destiny

Life is full of twists and turns along with obstacles
Nevertheless, how you survive them is to take chances
And make the best of every occasion as your last
Because who knows if it will ever happen again
That is why as I got older I became more relentless
Because I only live once and I'm not promised tomorrow
Therefore, when I want something I go for it no matter what
As life can pass you over with the blink of an eye
Because what I feel for you is tremendously real
And I am willing to make you my Destiny

Feel Used

No matter what I do, I cannot figure out women
I know they say that only women understand women
However, I seem to get lost in between what women want
Because no matter how sweet they say I am
I continue to be overlooked for someone else
And I cannot comprehend what is wrong with me
To have this happen to me over and over again
It just shatters my hopes and dreams to be happy
Because no one wants to be alone forever
As I hate to feel used

Every time I meet a new woman, it starts out great
And I am myself from start to finish
Because as they say your first impression could be your last
And I always represent the man that I was born to be
Yet I continue to get the short end of the stick
I am not saying that I am perfect but deserve a fair chance
I even have tried to let women come find me
Even then, it seems to back fire for the worse
As I cannot figure out this displeasure that comes my way
Because it just makes me feel used

Day by day, I sit and explore what I need to change
And I have come to the conclusion to make things better
Because I just refuse to continue down this shallow path
And I know that settling down is not in the cards for me
I will not have to worry about that after the publication of my book
Because my blessing will be granted for me to survive
And from that point on in my life I will be free
Because I will only need to pay attention to myself
As I try not to allow these excruciating demons
That causes women to pass me by in life
Continue to make me feel used

Finish Last

Losing is just a phase in life for some people
But where it stands out the most is for nice guys
Because no women will look in their direction
And for guys like this it plays tricks on their mind
As you begin to question yourself as a man
Because no matter what you do for a woman
It gives you the impression that you're not worthy
To be loved for being nice and giving your all
As the saying goes nice guys finish last

There is no handbook to prepare you for this
Prepping for rejection and being used can't be taught
And being treated this way is like being picked last
In everything you do from high school dances and sports
Nothing is ever in your favor no matter how hard you try
Because all the hurdles you encounter dampens the heart
All the way to the core of your soul's existence
Because nice guys always finish last

All I can say fellas don't give up on yourself
Because at the end of the day God has your back
As long as you maintain your faith in Him
His plan for you in life is greater than anything
That you can ever encounter and go through
And when that perfect woman comes to you
Not only will you be that nice guy in her life
But the love of her life forever and ever
As you will become her never-ending love
And her number one guy that will finish last

Frightened

We have been talking to one another daily
As our conversations have been incredible
Because we have been through a lot in our lives
You are unsure if you can start over in life
Because you have been in a relationship for years
However, you want to venture out and explore the world
When you decided to take that chance
As you watched me walk past the lingerie store
Because you thought, I looked interesting and fun
You figured you had nothing to lose
Because you wanted to step into the light again
While escaping the feeling of being frightened

You rushed out of lingerie store with your girlfriend
As you followed me into J. Riggins for men
When I passed by the dress ties display you said hello
As our eyes met, it was as if time stood still around us
And I was speechless of the vision that was in front of me
Because the sparkle of your smile caught me off guard
As I said hello back as I cleared the frog from my throat
While the store light seemed to get hotter by the minute
As my nerves started to make me bead up with sweat
And it felt like I was stuck in quicksand and could not move
As your girlfriend noticed and laughed walking away
I finally snapped out of it and introduced myself
While escaping the feeling of being frightened

Give Up on You

I hear voices inside my heart calling for help
Nevertheless, I cannot figure out why oh why
My heart is speaking to my soul
Because I thought, I had found the one
However, more and more I feel lost with her
Because I don't know if it's real or fake
And I want her to talk about me as the one
That will bring her joy when she is sad
And lift her up when she is down
Because I feel, she is special to me
But with the voices inside clouding my mind
I just want to give up on you!

I keep wondering if this is what you want
Because it seems like you're clueless at times
And a relationship is not your strong suit
Because you seem to attract the clowns in life
As you keep putting your heart on the line
To just get sucked into lackluster love
Because you give it your all and they use you
However, you stick around and hope it improves
And as time slips away you lose faith
However, you cannot blame anyone but yourself for it
Even though I want to be the one for you
All I can do to save myself is give up on you!

Godmother

My Godmother is one of a kind
You just imagine
How special she is to me
Throughout her lifetime
She has made a name for herself
By single-handedly raising her Godchildren
While she worked to put food on the table
And clothes on our backs
As she keeps a roof over our heads
And manages to keep us on the right path
She should receive an award
For her effort and good will
Just for being our Godmother

Although I'm one of the godchildren
I wish her the best and much more
Because you are my #1 role model
Of all times because I love you
And the intelligence you possess
Along with the wisdom you demonstrate
I hope you pass onto me one day
Therefore, I can share with my children
And also, my own grandchildren
As I explain to them how wonderful
That my Godmother was to me
For being a part of my life
It always brings tears to my eyes
Because you're my Godmother

It makes me the happiest godchild in the world
Just knowing God blessed me with you
And that I am your biggest fan
But saying this isn't enough for me
I hope that as time passes by
You bless me with your talent and skills
To be as lovely as you
I cannot imagine the day
When I can make you so proud of me
Knowing deep inside my heart
You will always watch over me
Because of your big heart
And caring soul for me
I can only wish that I did you proud
Because you're my Godmother

When I look back upon the past
I will always see your pretty smile
No matter how bad things get in my life
I will gather the strength of your love
To help me through rough times
That I may encounter in my future
However, I cannot think of anyone
That can ever take your place in my heart
Because you're my Godmother

Greatest Gift

As the cruise ship docks in the Bahamas
And the smell of the island food is in the air
I watch, the blue seas run over the white sands
As I exit the ship and approach the grounds
As the cool breeze blows through the trees
And the sunrays beam upon my silky skin
Because this trip is what I needed to clear my head
As the music captivates the essence of my soul
And the sound of the island music moves me
As it brings my heart to a standstill
Because of my every thought of you
Will always be my Greatest Gift

Only God can judge me for my wrongful doing
Because he has produced this pain in my heart
As I stand out on the balcony in the island breeze
I look down below and picture you lying in the sand
As my mouth begins to water with the very sight of you
Because all I can imagine is you in my arms
As we lay in the sand with our bodies pressed together
While the water from the sea trickles down our skin
As the burning desire divulges in our eyes
Because you will always be my Greatest Gift

Half Crazy

I felt as though I was losing my mind
Because of the pain I was feeling inside
I know that the pain was not easy for you
However, I can tell you I am sorry forever
And it still won't make things better
However, I realize now what I am missing
With you not in my life anymore
Because that makes me Half Crazy

It has not been much fun since you have been gone
And the pain that I have caused you
Comes at a price that I am paying for
Nevertheless, so you know I still love you
As I always will but I know it is over
Because you made that very clear
Therefore, you know I will never stop loving you
But if holding on to those feelings
Will do my soul more damage than good
I will prefer to let you go
And not make myself Half Crazy

Handsome Specimen

As I get out of the shower to prepare for tonight
I pick up the phone to call all my single ladies
Because the day has come for our monthly outing
As we all meet at my house and wait for our limo
We get dressed in our finest outfits to impress
And slowly each lady arrives one by one
As we follow our ritual and make a toast to the night
Just as we finish our champagne, the limo pulls up
As we head toward the door, we grab our purses
And we all have a laugh as we approach the limo
We all have to do a double take at the limo driver
Because he is a handsome specimen

As we each entered the limo with cottonmouth
Because what we are witnessing, is a good-looking man
As he helped us into the limo, you could hear a pin drop
Because we were all blown away with his appeal
And the politeness of this fine gentleman driver
As we all began to comment and whisper about him
I needed him to notice me and only me right now
Because I felt so childish just thinking about him
As I wanted to know everything I could about him
Just hoping he was a single man as I am a single woman
Because I never lost control over a male ever in my life
However, this man seems so much different from men of my past
Because he is a handsome specimen

Haunted Past

We have been working on us for quite some time now
And we started on the right foot from the beginning
But as time has went on it seems we are at a crossroad
And I just do not know what to do with my lost emotions
Because I have poured every ounce of my soul into you
And it seems like you have still not let go of the past
As it has driven a wedge in between our hearts
Because it has caused me to feel sad all over again
And I vowed not to allow myself to go backwards
However, I promised myself to continue to move forward
And all of this has come at a price to my heart
Because you are still holding on to your Haunted Past

You have caused confusion in my mind I cannot stand
And it has me going in circles about our relationship
Because you have made it difficult to hang on to us
However, I need to step back and focus on me
Because all in all I have to protect my welfare
And not be sucked back into the darkness again
As I have been told that things are never perfect in life
Nevertheless, you made me forget all those imperfections
That life can throw at you and bring to the surface
Because I never could have imagined it to hurt so bad
And our feelings for each other seemed so priceless
As I begin to cave in from what I'm feeling
Because you are still holding onto your Haunted Past

When I see you, I become happy and sad all at once
However, I know it is the pain flowing through my veins
And it will get worse until you let go of the past
Because until then we cannot build on the future
And I know that God made it a point for us to meet
I just think that the ghost of your past has you captured
And I have been willing to help you release those demons
However, as you get close to letting go you grip tighter to the past
And it seems that you are hanging off a cliff
Because you want to let go but are afraid to do so
And it increases the distance more & more between us
Because you continue to hold on to your Haunted Past

I have realized that it is time for me to do me
And that means to step away from you for awhile
Because I can't afford to get lost in love again
And you must understand that this is hard for me
Nevertheless, I have to do this for us if we can survive together
Now you must find within your soul freedom if you want me
Because I will provide you the time to find your true feelings
And it may never blossom into what we could have had
However, I gave it my all through every bump in the road for us
Because what I felt for you seemed so right in my heart
And it made me come out of my shell to love again
I think your past is too dark for you to overcome inside
Because you can't shake your Haunted Past

I am Broken

Life filled with joy and pain, in and out of love
I have finally lost my sanity with my soul
Because the darkness has covered my heart
As my protective walls are crumbling down
With each passing day, the pain is relentless
As my tears have turned into a sand storm
Because my weeping tears have become a mirage
As I try to stand tall on shaky legs
With the throbbing of my lost soul inside
Because me finding true love has depreciated
As I know for a fact I am Broken

Whoever said women want a caring and loving man
That is an old wive's tale from a fantasy world
Because when you are that type of man
It does not matter if you are sweet and kind
Even if that's the man God has made you
That is a sweet, caring, big-hearted man
No one is perfect except for our Heavenly Father
He has blessed me with a unique soul and heart
However, women take that for granted
I know for a fact because I am Broken

I know that you can experience love more than once
However, with the bad luck I carry with women
It makes it seem impossible and not feasible for me
Because the heartache of a lost marriage and girlfriends
Tells my story from within explaining my dejection
With all of the sorrow and pain I have endured
I have to wonder if being alone is my destiny
Because with this pain I am Broken

I Don't Like

We had something special going on between us in our lives
However, it all began to unravel in the blink of an eye
Because just when our good times turned to bad
I wanted to go somewhere and hide for an eternity
Because I made you the cornerstone in my heart
And you brought that cornerstone crumbling down
As I felt safe in your presence inside my dreams
And you tarnished my soul with your cold heart
Because all I did was make you my everlasting love
And the pain was carved deep into my self-esteem
As I thought I had finally made the correct choices
And what I'm feeling I Don't Like

All my life I have been chasing after the woman of my life
And I thought for the first time that the one found me
But as we started out on the highest pedestal together
You caused me to fall into the shadows of the dark
Because I believed in you and what you showed me
And it made me let my guard down to trust you
Because I never felt this way about anyone before
As I was destined to give you all of me for life
And you could not just accept the gift of love from me
You had to go and crush the unlocked love I had inside
Because that feeling is what I Don't Like

Repeatedly in my mind, I hear your heartbeat
However, it keeps my spirits within my soul restless
I cannot get you out of my everyday thoughts
Because what we had was extremely special
It made my love soar over the moon at night
And climb up tall mountains without a rope
But as you threw my love out the window
With your acts of depression and betrayal
I have learned a valuable lesson during this
When you wear your heart on your sleeve
And with the slightest touch it can be crushed
Because when you get that feeling inside
It causes misery in every bone in your body
And that feeling I Don't Like

I Won't Stand in Your Way

Life is too short to waste time on me forever
So, finding out you are looking for happiness
Is something I want for you in your life?
So, knowing you are not satisfied with us
I will give you your desired exit pass
For you to be happy I must let you go
You want things that I cannot provide you
And with all of the other handsome guys
You are talking to and interested in
I understand the distance we have had recently
So, baby you are free to move on
Not that you needed my permission you're grown
I hope that you find your true love in the future
And have the world at your feet on a platter
Because I won't stand in your way!

Just Because

I have a warm feeling coming over me
As it just touches my soul
Because I reminisce about you in my mind
And those thoughts make me shake my head
Because what I'm thinking just can't be true
As I always dreamed of the moment to have you
Because I knew I could make you really happy
However, the challenges ahead can cause family drama
But you are oh so worth every bit of the fuss
Because I always had strong feelings for you
I just cannot explain what you do to me just because

The new waters we would be treading will be rough
Nevertheless, I will go down with the ship
Because I feel that strongly about you and me
Nobody will stand in the way if we have each other
Because true happiness is just a fingertip away
That is something we can definitely have together
I will be all the man that you are missing
Because we had to go through our difficult ordeals
For both of us to get to this point to be together
Because you only get to live once in life
And you drive me wild just because

Last Breath

As I look at this picture of you my ladylove
I fall deeper and deeper in love with you
Because you have captivated my soul
With your intelligence and beauty
And I can't imagine not loving you
You have given me hope again in life
And I am truly blessed to be with you
Because God has granted me your hand
To comfort me, to love me and be mine
I pray that you will let me be yours forever
And my every thought of you blows my mind
Because you have sparked my flame
That I felt would never light again
But with God's help you lit the torch to my soul
And I am truly grateful for you being my new wick
That has got my fire burning hotter and hotter again
I love you more and more from sunup to sundown
And will love you forever until my very last breath

Last Kiss

I understand what you are feeling inside
But I know this is the end for us after our talk
And losing a love is something I have felt before
Because it is never a wholesome feeling to cope with
And I am not making excuses for what happened in the past
All I can say is I am truly sorry for your pain
I know I cannot change the past but only change the future
And with that being said I wish you joy in life
I have always wanted more for you than you know
And now listening to your heart in our conversation
It seems that what I bring to the table is less of a man
Because you need something more than I was made to offer
But today I celebrate your milestone birthday with you
And I pray to God that you enjoy this day he granted you
You only live once in this crazy world of today
And I hope that this becomes a memory for you
Whether you include me as part of this day or not
I understand where your heart is and needs to be
Take what I am about to say for what it is worth
I do love you and I love you dearly my love
I'm not going to block your dreams for happiness
Loving you was an honor and my pleasure
I pray you find what you want in life forever
Because the hardest thing is that last kiss

Left Behind

The world is a cruel place to live in
However, when God has something in place
And in mind that you need to survive
He will bless you with an abundance of joy
You have been hurt repeatedly
But your faith has not been destroyed
You keep standing tall no matter what
And you never will be Left Behind

Recently you have met someone that attracts you
And you do not know how to pursue him
However, you need to allow yourself to feel safe
Because he feels strongly about you
And it just breaks his heart to see you hurting
You mean just so much to him deep down inside
He walks with his heart on his sleeve for you
And will protect you any way shape or form
Because he doesn't want you Left Behind

Loving Me

I have been yearning for someone special
And finding that person hasn't been easy
However, you have come into my life
Just like a cool summer breeze
With a heart of gold
And that heart-stopping smile
However, you have been a God sent to me
As I am thankful to have you in my life
And for you just loving me

I want to provide you with the world
And be the man that you can count on
Through all the good and bad times
Because we both have had broken hearts
And we both deserve to have happiness
Because our hearts are calling for bliss
And every time I see your smile, it shows
Because we are good for one another in many ways
And I am willing to find out how good it can be
Because you are the one, I see loving me

Lust for You

I cannot wait to see you in the morning
Because each day you bring joy to my life
With each passing hour, I think of you
However, very soon I will be in your arms
Holding, kissing and squeezing you tight
Because I never knew love like this
Until you walked into my tedious life
With every gentle touch of your fingertips
As they stroked my silky brown skin
And caused my muscles to tense up inside
Because that makes me Lust for You

My life was in ruins until you rescued me
Because I couldn't find my way anymore
As I thought, the end was near for me
Then you salvaged my inner core from despair
With your spoken words of wisdom
Because you see the pain on my face
Along with the excruciating sound in my voice
And all you wanted to do at first was cry
However, you knew that your tears would not help
Because you wanted me to stand strong
As your caring nature makes me Lust for You

Marry Me

I know I have not shown you my feeling in the past
However, if I was to lose you I would go crazy
So, with this opportunity for a second chance
I want you to know that I will embrace you
As my ladylove, lover, baby, and my wife to be
I missed you every second and thought you were gone forever
Because I didn't fight for you like my soul cried for you
And spending the weekend with you opened my soul
To speak out to you and tell you what you mean to me
And it felt so good to say I Love U all over again
What I feel for you I want to feel to the end of time
I pray that you grant me the wish to be yours
And I will acknowledge to the world I am yours
Because I Love you now, always and forever
And someday soon I want you to Marry Me!

Mouthwatering

The time has finally come for us to meet in person
If you knew the feeling of the butterflies I have inside
Because a part of me still gets shy around pretty women
And I truly think you are one of those astonishing women
So, if I have a hard time looking you in your eyes at first
It is because my shyness and butterflies are running wild
However, it only lasts for awhile before I can gaze into your eyes
And read what you have going on deep within your soul
Because what you have inside of you I feel is extremely special
And I would love to get to know you from inside out
As we spend time together this weekend for hours and hours
I am excited to be able to escort you to your special event
Because walking with you on my arm is going to be an honor
That I will cherish and lock away in my memory banks
And to see you all dressed up will make me bow down to you
As I will worship and cherish the ground you walk on
Because as I sit here and write this I just get the chills
Just to see how truly beautiful you will be in person
My heart is beating fast just thinking about it
And these feelings I am experiencing are mouthwatering

My Soul is Lost

Heavenly Father, forgive me for the horrible thoughts
Because what I am feeling right now hurts deep down
And no matter how much I laugh or shed tears
I cannot shake the crumbling of my heart and soul
And my body is numb like I was injected with novocaine
As my pores are oozing with sadness and pain
Because my love has moved on with me still around
And nothing can explain what that feels like inside
But what I do know is my soul is lost

Life can leave a good and a bad taste in your mouth
And to suffer with that stabbing pain within
Can cause your mind to go into darkness with ease
And the devil will prey on those insecurities developing
Because he waits for that perfect moment to strike
And when he gets ahold of you it can spell the end
As you give in to the burning fire of his grasp
Because he knows my soul is lost

God, please save me from these life altering thoughts
Because my mind, body and soul has weakened
As I feel like it is time to surrender to him forever
And just go away from being a burden for others
My life has never been what you wanted it to be
And no matter the impression I project to people
It just cannot outweigh the shadows in the night
That has incarcerated this large heart of mine
Because I truly know my soul is lost

My Soul Will Be Free

As I wipe away the tears of my pain running down my face
I grab my pad and pen to write down my last thoughts
Because my doctor has told me I don't have much time left
And all that my soul can muster is all the memories in my heart
That made me smile, laugh, cry and drop to my knees
But to all my family, friends and enemies I want you to know
That I will miss you and take your love along with me
Because my life has been a merry-go-round of happiness
And each of you played a major role in that part of my life
To be a man of faith and to know God has taken the wheel
As he preps my place with him into his loving arms
Because coming soon in my life my soul will be free

I don't know if I have minutes, hours or days here on earth
But what I do know is that my heart and soul is at peace
And there is never a moment in a day that I don't thank God
Not for what I have achieved, but how he allowed me to survive
And I will always be grateful, humble and truly blessed
Through all my life's ups and downs on this journey
Because I was created in my Heavenly Father's image
And that in its own right shows me how much he loves me
As I prepare for my last breath of my very existence
I close my eyes and thank each of you in my prayers
Because each tear I shed proves that my soul will be free

P.A.T.L. (Precious All Time Love)

I know things have been rocky between us my dear
But I am truly trying to work on just our future
I know I'm not the normal type of guy you date or love
But just so you know I want you and only you
Because I was scared for years and doubted myself with you
And I know excuses won't change the hurt within
I am trying to be that guy you fell in love with all along
It may be too late for me to salvage you and me
But I will ride it out until our train stops at the end
And no matter where the train ends I will love you
Until I take my last breath and hold onto our memories
My P.A.T.L. (Precious All Time Love)

Precious Gem

I know you feel I don't want to be here with you
But I haven't wanted to be anywhere but here
Because I have never felt love as strong as this
Even through other relationships and marriages
And sometimes it scares me to feel this way
But I am not running from this love we have
Because to you it seems I take it for granted
But I am going to change that tarnished feeling
And try to make you want me every day
As I want you in my life forever and ever
Because you are my precious gem

Saving Grace

Just as the dark clouds begin to cover the sky
And I reach for a tissue to dry my eye
Because your gentle voice is ringing in my head
As the tears build up in my eyes it makes me blind
Because you are my star that shines bright
And the moon that lights the sky in the night
With the rain starting to fall upon my window pane
As I stare out into the storm looking silly
Because you have given me life in so many ways
As you will always be my Saving Grace

Only God can control things for all of us
Because he knows what we go through in a flash
And in a pinch, he gave me your amazing love
Because you fit the mold that was meant to be
And he made you perfect so I could see
You every time I go to pray and take a knee
I cherish the love of my life that was meant to be
As I will reminisce over the life that was given to us
You will always be the best thing that ever happened to me
Because you are my Saving Grace

Sorry!

You seem to be distant lately
I hope you are not mad at me
Because if you are I don't know why
Whatever it is please let me know
Because I can feel you slipping away
That is not what I want
However, it is not up to me to make that choice
Just so, you know I am Sorry!

I will do whatever it takes to make things right
However, until I know the situation my hands are tied
Can you open up and tell me what is wrong?
And if I have caused you any displeasure
I am Sorry!

You know you are my sun and my moon
That brightens my days and nights
Knowing you are unhappy breaks my heart
If I can change anything at all let me know
Because I will do anything to make it right
Just so, you know I am Sorry!

Stranded

As I listen to the wind blow outside my window
And watch the pretty fall leaves drop to the ground
As I fade into the depths of my soul
Because I know that I am lost in love
And I know that I will never love again
Because of my last relationship's sorrows
And it has made me just give up on women
Because true love is not possible for me
And love seems to bring me pain
Nevertheless, just when I think it is true I get hurt
As my heart begins to feel stranded

All my life I dreamed of getting married
And having the perfect life with my wife
However, each time I fall in love
Because of the way, they made me feel
As I wore my heart on my sleeve
And that was dangerous to my soul
Because they would break my heart
And it made my soul weak inside
Because of how I was treated
And my heart feels stranded

This last heartbreak was the last straw
And my homies held me together
As they brought me up to the cabin
Because they felt that I needed to get away
And this trip would provide me with sanity
Nevertheless, all I could do is think of my pain
Because I knew I could never love again
As I sit and watch the leaves fall down
And my life's dreams begin to fade
However, my homies try to cheer me up
Because they hate to see me in pain
And it kills them to see me this way
Because they know, I feel stranded

Sweet Kisses

I am at a loss for words but let me clear my mind
And tell you what my soul is quivering about
Because with those long golden blonde locks
And those provocative sweet luscious lips
As I gaze deep into those enchanting eyes
Which makes my mouth water in extreme lust
As I want to hold you close in my arms
And kiss you until I'm out of breath
Because I can't get enough of your sweet kisses

As I gently run my fingers through your hair
And the pleasant aroma of your fragrance
Lingers in the air with my fixation for you
Which has my heart-beating heavy upon my skin
As my body goes numb from deep within
Because you have this tender touch
That makes my muscles weak from head to toe
And what I feel is mesmerizing to my soul
Dreaming of those passionate sweet kisses

The Next Generation

What has this world become for our kids?
Remember the days of jump rope, hide & seek
Red light green light, jacks, hopscotch
Tag and the list goes on and on
Those were the good old days
When we could play outside all day and all night
And our parents had no worries in the world
But in today's society it scares them to death
Always wondering if this maybe the last time
They will see their kids for just one more hug
Or that last kiss, or get to say I Love You
This nonsense has to stop and save our future
For our kids and grandkids the next generation

Treasure Chest

Our 2nd journey together has started out rocky
But one of the most enjoyable things is our love
And I know I'm not the most established person
But I will do whatever God allows me to do
To be the greatest man I can be always and forever
And words can't explain my love I feel for you
Because I have allowed that same love to consume me
As it has made my own insecurities stunt our growth
And I just want to say that I am truly SORRY
Because I don't want to destroy our love again
And I will do whatever it takes to make things right
You have a hold on my soul that I want to cherish
And if I destroy these feelings I will never forgive myself
So, I want you in my life until my last God-given breath
Because you have reeled in my heart with your love
And your love has engraved its imprint on my soul
Because of this superb feeling I have inside for you
I give my soul to you because it is now your Treasure Chest

Twinkle in Her Eye

As the alarm clock goes off
I see that the sun is shining bright
And it looks to be a beautiful day
As I get prepared to go for my run
I grab my keys and head outside
As I begin to stretch on the curb
And I hit play on my phone
I begin my daily jog
As I feel someone staring at me
And I continue down the street
As you finally catch my attention
With the twinkle in her eye

As I pass by her sitting on the bench
I smile over to her and wave
She begins to wave back putting me in a daze
With her amazingly beautiful smile
That completely stopped me in my tracks
As I head over to introduce myself
She seems to blush with my every step
And I cannot help but notice all of her beauty
Because it would stand out in a crowd
Especially today on this summer day
With the twinkle in her eye

Chapter 2

ANGELS

As Dove's Fly

Heavenly Father, give my family the strength to be at peace
Because my life was filled with everlasting love
And I will always treasure my life's blessings
As you have stood by me through all my ups and downs
I ask that you hold my family and friends in your arms
So they can cherish the memories we shared together
And not shed many tears from their souls over me
Because I know you have a plan for me as I come home
To be with you inside your glorious kingdom of heaven
And spread my angel wings As Dove's Fly

In Loving Memory of Patricia C. Moore

Darling Momma

Life is full of surprises with highs and lows
As you raised me from a child to a woman
You made all of my days become highs
With your beautiful smile that lit up a room
Along with your wonderful personality
You filled my life everyday with joy & compassion
Because of you I was able to grow as a woman
God blessed me with an angel such as you
I am truly grateful that you are my Mother
Because I love you more with each passing day
You made my dreams come true every second of my life
No matter how bad things seemed you always wore a smile
And it made me feel safe and untouchable to evil
Because you made my foundation strong
With your soft-spoken conversation speeches
Along with BIG HUGS & Kisses when I was sad and blue
Because you knew the remedy to lift my spirits
I will always remember the times we shared
Because you etched memories in my soul
And only God can take them away from me
However, he just keeps adding more to my soul
Because God provided me with you in my life
As I am truly thankful and extremely blessed
Because I had you with me through the years
I love you always & forever my Darling Momma!

"In Loving Memory of Diane Bruce"

E.R.I.N. (Elegant Royalty In Nature)

I know today has been tough on family and friends
But God called you home because he needed you more
And he blessed you with your angel wings in heaven
No matter how much we shed tears of sorrow for you
We will never forget your pretty smile and big heart
Because you touched our souls beyond the stars
With kindness, love and care from morning to night
And tonight we kneel down to pray united together
As God etches your spirit deep inside our souls forever
Because we know you are already looking down on us
And we thank you for always being a part of our lives
We miss you already and our hearts are heavy with grief
This is never goodbye, this is I will see you again
R.I.P. our Elegant Royalty In Nature

Family Love

Memories are cherished within the depths of the soul
As my heartbreaks thinking about your beautiful smile
Because you were my best friend, confidant and rock
As the years past by I still hear the sound of your voice
And the soothing melody that it made inside my heart
Because it made me feel safe and warm from head to toe
And the chills within the nucleus of my soul is incredible
Because that feeling is the bond we shared together
And that is called Family Love

In Loving Memory of Marlene Bradley

Fly Away

God wraps his loving arms around my saddened soul
And his warm touch comforts my weeping heart
As his heart beats, steadily in sync with mine
And the softness of his voice lifts my spirit
Letting me know that he will never forsake me
Because he has provided you with angel wings
And that he has appointed you my guardian angel
So, my tears of sorrow will turn into tears of joy
Because your spirit lives on inside me forever
Just like the flowers blooming in the spring
And the stars shine bright in the night
Mr. Torrey Sutton, you touched me deeply
And my love for you will never fade away
Because God will shine his joyful light upon me
As he lets me know that you're with me always
And that my guardian angel will never fly away!

In Loving memory of "Torrey Sutton"

God Has My Soul

The battle is over with cancer, because God has called me home
Please don't cry for me, because I have won the war am now at peace
God has a better plan for me now to look down upon you
And provide your spirit with comfort and love to see you through
All of the daily trials of missing me, but to lift your heart with memories
This is not goodbye it is just I will see you later in God's kingdom
Where we can embrace each other with lots of hugs and laughter
As we walk the path inside of the gates of heaven with God
Because we will be free from all of the world's suffering and pain
I know this is hard on you to swallow right now that I'm gone
But my spirit lives on more powerful than any disease on earth
And I know that God's loving grace has guided me to a better place
My life has been good to me, but God Has My Soul

In Loving Memory of "Carolyn Rupp"

God in Heaven

Hello family may God comfort your soul and spirit
Because he has called me home for eternity
And to you it feels like it was too soon
But his plan for me is beyond my wildest dreams
Because he has granted me my angel wings
So, I can watch over each of you until we meet again
And God's blessings is something I will cherish
As I am able to comfort your mind as you sleep
With all the fond memories we shared as a family
And my love for each of you will conquer all pain
Because I am standing tall with God in Heaven

In Loving Memory of Viola E. "Vi" Purnell

Heaven's Love

I've climbed many mountains in my lifetime with you
And God created you and me to become united as one
As the angels were singing and the doves soared above
Because we stood upon God's throne and said I do
We cherished every moment of our lives together
And right now, I ask that you thank God for our love
Because this is not the end it is just the beginning
Don't you shed tears of sadness shed tears of joy
As God will keep me safe in his arms until we meet again
Because he has kept his promise to me with Heaven's Love

In Loving Memory of Joyce D. Lewis Hunter
Our thoughts and prayers from the Brown, Williams & Witcher Family!

Love Everlasting

Blessings come in all ways of life unimaginable
And God granted you to me Dan as the love of my life
As your love for me lifted my spirit within my heart
And the twinkle in your eyes always lit my spark
Because when you hugged me I felt so secure
And when you kissed me I felt my heartbeat pure
As God made our 24 years together last forever
And to share it with you made it that much better
Because our love is so strong that it weathered the storm
As I will miss you dearly my Love Everlasting!

In loving memory of "Daniel Webster Stayathome"

Mighty Clouds of Joy

As you remember our lives as you kneel to pray
Let our infectious smiles dry your tears
And the wonderful memories bring you joy
Because this is not goodbye this is I will see you later
As I will be waiting for you when the time comes
So, we can share laughs, kisses and hugs once again
And don't cry for me because I am home in Heaven
Where you and me will walk among the King of Kings
One day together without sorrow, pain and prejudice
Because God has comforted us deep within his arms
As we walk amongst the Mighty Clouds of Joy

In Loving Memory of Ruth and Kitty

Mom, Dad & Sis

Mom, Dad & Sis please don't cry God is holding me now
Tight in his arms as he sprinkles blessing upon me
As he allowed me to blossom inside you mom
Alongside my sister sharing amazing moments
And for that I am grateful to our Heavenly Father
For making me a part of a magnificent family forever
I may not be here physically but my spirit is strong
As God promises to us all we will meet again
Without any trials and tribulations in our lives
And I have a BIG HUG for each of you on that day
Because I was a miracle of God and part of both of you
Please, hold onto the memories of me as a blessing
And not of sadness and heartache Mom, Dad & Sis

In Loving Memory of Gabriella Faith

My Spirit Free

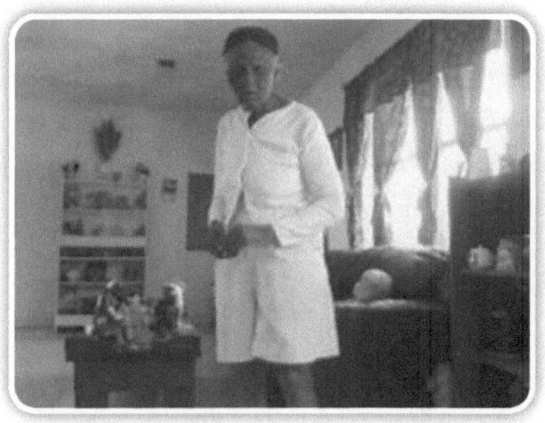

Spring showers are falling upon my broken heart
As my tears for you run down my face
And my mind wanders with memories of you
Because each tear has a story for us to share
As they roll off my skin in pure sadness
Because I know God blessed me with you
And that is a treasure that makes gold worthless
Because your heart was big and strong with passion
And that is a love that touched my soul within
I know you will shine your light upon my life
And keep me safe within your angel wings
As your love for me has set my spirit free

In Loving Memory of you Grandma "Lois Monts Witcher"

No One like You

When I was small you held me in your arms
As you rocked me back and forth to sleep
And it felt so good to be held by you
Because as I grew you continued to hold me
And I felt like the luckiest granddaughter in the world
You taught me to live, love and laugh each day
Your guidance and strength helped mold me
The soft whisper of your voice soothed my soul
Your passionate kisses made me value family
And with the sacrifices you made taught me about life
As I treasure the love you gave to me as a child
God has lifted my spirit in honor of your life
He provided me a grandmother second to none
And I know you are in a better place right now
Always looking down on me with that great smile
Letting me know that things will be just fine
And with you watching over me every passing day
I love you Grandmom Maria Rios my guardian angel
As I know in my heart there is no one like you!

"In Loving Memory of Maria Rios"

Queen of My Heart

Don't let my passing dishearten your soul
Because I will greet you at Heaven's pearly gates
And remember I am not gone I was just called home
With my angel wings and my energetic smile
While I stand here next to our Lord and Savior
As Heaven's sun shines, bright upon you
Please, don't shed any tears of sadness over me
And when you get a chill inside it's just me hugging you
With my strong arms wrapped around you Pat
As my heart is missing you and prancing in my chest
While the blood in my veins flows with our love
Because my darling Pat you are the Queen of my Heart

In Loving Memory of Al

Rebecca Ann Taylor

Sadness has brought us together as a family
But God has comforted us with your spirit
Because Rebecca you blessed us in many ways
With your smile, kindness and loving personality
God works in mysterious ways in our lives
And he graced us with your presence daily
Because if you look up the word strength
Your picture would be shown next to the word
And God gave you wings to be our Angel
Because your strength held us together
During your toughest times of need
And I am truly grateful to be your sister
I will truly miss you always and forever
And my love for you is etched in my soul
Because God has set you free from pain
And made you the family Angel
I miss you and love you Rebecca!

In Loving Memory of 'Rebecca Ann Taylor"

Remembering You Auntie

As the night unfolds and the stars shine bright above
I look toward the heavens just to know that you're gone
And my sadness is weighing heavy upon my soul
Because you loved me like I was your daughter
And only you could keep secrets like a sister or best friend
My love for you overshadows the pain that I'm feeling
But, don't think for one minute I'm not missing you dearly
My mornings are dark and my nights are filled with tears
I miss you more than my spoken words can ever express
Because I will love you always from the depths of my soul!

My Thoughts and Prayers for you April Hofacker

Remembering You Mom

As the wind blows and the sun shines on my skin
There is never a day that passes by that I don't miss you
Every year gets harder and harder since you've been gone
But I know God's greatest angel is looking down on me
As the thought of you makes tears run down my face
Because God graced me with the most remarkable mother
And the love I have for you makes me miss you dearly
As my heart and soul cries out to the heavens above
And prays for you to hold me close one more time
As I close my eyes to imprison our memories together
And the thing I will cherish the most is remembering you Mom!

In Loving Memory of Gwen C. DiNicola

Shining Star

God has called home the world's greatest angel
Because he created you to be my guide in life
And with you gone it hurts deep in my soul
But, God has swooped down into my heart
To ease my pain with joy and happiness
As he coats my spirit with your everlasting love
Because he knows you will never be forgotten
And that our memories will last until we meet again
Because you are still looking down upon me
As your warm touch caresses my soul
And for every tear I shed your spirit wipes them away
I know time will heal all the wounds in my heart
Just knowing you will be my eternal Shining Star

In loving memory of my Big Sister Linda

Spirit in Heaven

Hello family, I see the sadness on your faces right now
But so you don't lose faith with me being gone
Look deep inside your hearts and hear my voice
God and I will touch your souls with our grace
And begin to heal and protect you from all this pain
Because our Heavenly Father has called me home
So, don't question his reasoning just praise his choice
As my love will never fade away inside your hearts
Because God has lifted my Spirit in Heaven

In Loving Memory of Anthony Scarbro
My thoughts and prayers go out to The Scarbro Family

Temple of the Lord

I stare upon the stars that shine in the night
As I kneel down upon my knees and pray for you
While I reminisce of all the times we shared
And my tears begin to run like the river Jordan
As God sends his heavenly angels down to comfort me
And the light from your star shines upon my face
While the warmth of the light strengthens my spirit
Knowing that my pain is deep within my core
As God's angels help heal the void left in my heart
I miss you every day that you are not here with me
But God has etched you deep within my soul to keep
As you rest in peace in the Temple of the Lord

In loving memory of "Clinton Fields Jr."

True Angel

Looking upon the clouds as the doves soar high
While a sturdy wind blows upon my face
As my eyes begin to shut to hold back my tears
Just as the tears release from my eyes and down my face
I hear the whisper of your soft voice telling me it is ok
As I open my eyes I see the image of you in the clouds
Standing there so beautiful and at peace
As God has presented you with your angel wings
Because he has opened the gates and called you home
We miss you more than any words can validate
However, with the love you bestowed on us all
It will never be replaced and will never be forgotten
Because your gentle smile brightens my life
And when I was sad you gave me a loving hug
As it made my grey skies turn sunny and bright
And with you being a part of my life was a blessing
And God blessed us with a True Angel!

"In Loving Memory of Twyla Wilson"

Winds of My Sail

Jaden and Marvin, I feel your heartbeats in my arms
Because as every day passes I hold you both tight
As my spirit flows deep within your souls
And God's strong arms give me comfort
To let me know that his love is everlasting
And that he has granted me my wings to soar
As I share our life stories with our Heavenly Father
Because he knows how much you both miss me
And I want you to know I miss you both too
As this glorious holiday season is upon you
Just know that your number 1 girl is a prayer away
And I love you both from the depths of my soul
As I send you my best wishes, love and prayers
While you both are the Winds of my Sail

In Loving Memory of Jackie

Chapter 3
BUNDLES OF JOY

Baby Nova

Young love is one of the most precious things to see
And starting a family gives us goosebumps inside
Because our special bundle of joy will be here soon
And baby Nova has already hypnotized our hearts
Because she will be spoiled beyond a shadow of a doubt
From the top of her tiny head full of beautiful hair
All the way down to her precious little toes
Because our baby girl will secure our lives together
As we celebrate this journey with family and friends
And we can't wait to hear our baby Nova's first cry
So, we can hold you in our arms to keep you warm
As you open your eyes for a split second to see the world
And close them again to snuggle with mom and dad
Because God has blessed us with our baby Nova

Welcome baby Nova
Congratulations R J & Chelsea

Our Sweet Baby Girl

As I hold you in my arms for the first time
My heart melts with overflowing joy
And your precious face is breathtaking
As we cry together for the first time
And mommy and daddy's family is whole
Our priceless bundle of joy has arrived
And we will love you forever and ever
Our Sweet Baby Girl

Congratulations on the New Family Addition Tessa!

Wings to Soar in Heaven

So, beautiful, so precious, my heavenly angel
There are not enough words in the dictionary
That can express how I feel about you mom
Today is the start of my life without you
And I know God has called you home
But not having you here with me leaves a void
Because you were the glue in my life
And now I have to mend the crack in my soul
I know you are gazing down on me with a smile
As God has his arm around you for eternity
No matter how bad the storm you will be missed
And I will honor your life until we meet again
Loving you with all of my holy spirit
As you have earned your Wings to Soar in Heaven!

In Loving Memory of "Lois Monts Witcher"

With All My Heart

Hey my lovely daughter it's been years since I have passed
And I know your heart still hurts with me being gone
But you see this little bundle of joy I'm holding proudly
I passed on my spirit within my precious granddaughter
So, I can still be close and watch over you daily
Because I know her smile and spunk will keep you going
And I know our memories will continue to live in her
Just knowing you miss me makes our meeting again special
But for now, close your eyes and say a prayer for us
And listen to my heartbeat pound right next to yours
Because that is the sound of my spirit comforting your soul
As you begin to shed a tear of sadness that turns to joy
Because God will never leave us or forsake us
And my angel wings are waiting to hold you tight
Just like I did when you were a little girl growing up
I love you my darling with all my heart!

In Loving Memory of Mom Bruce

You're My Blessing

Vern, God blessed me with you always and forever
All my life I searched high and low for you
And on the greatest day of my life he delivered you
To me from the heavens above to comfort my soul
On that very day, my prayers and blessings came true
And my life has soared above the clouds ever since
Because God showed me the light to happiness
And that happiness was you becoming my wife
With you by my side I had the world and more
Your precious smile captivated my mind and soul
That made this grown man fall in love with you
And the love I had for you was extra special
Because every day I fell endlessly in love with you
I will love you always and forever Vern
Because you were my life long blessing from God!

In loving memory of "William Scott Cowan Jr."

Chapter 4

FESTIVITIES

Christmas Prayer to My Daughter

I know it has been 14 years since you last seen my face my daughter
But sitting here next to God looking down upon you this Christmas
Is a blessing to watch over you and see you happy with family!
I miss you and sharing the holiday season with you my dear
And I know you cannot see me but the warm feeling you feel
Are my warm arms around you with an enormous hug for you!
I wish you many, many more Christmases to share with family
As I hold back my tears and kneel down in prayer with God
Letting you know that I will always miss you and love you
This is my Christmas Prayer to my Daughter

In loving memory of "Dea J.B. Brown

Family Tree Christmas

Words are hard to put together with tears in your eyes
But that just goes to show what you mean to me
And with every passing day I am truly blessed with you
Because no matter what we go through mentally and physically
You seem to have a heart of gold for me in your soul
Which radiates deep inside of me when I am feeling blue
And that strength I find within during those moments lifts me up
Because I may not be the best nephew in this world
But God blessed me with you to always be in my corner
Whether I am right or wrong you provide words of wisdom
Thank you for being a part of my Family Tree Christmas

God Bless you this Christmas
Loving you for an eternity your Nephew

Happy 15th Anniversary

Here we stand today to celebrate our 15th Anniversary
As we reminisce through the years of pain and triumph
And as time has us positioned stronger than ever
Because God has blessed us with each other forever
And our growing love is built tough together
As our lives are intertwined like fine leather
Because nothing can destroy our love together
As we renew our vows to show the world forever
That we will add more years of our lives together
As we share this superb day with our family & friends forever!

Happy 15th Anniversary Mr. & Mrs. Ashlock
Love you both always and forever!

Happy 39th Valentine's Day Mark

What a time in our lives for us to be sharing 39yrs together
This is a tremendous feat to last through it all
But God has given me to you and you to me for eternity
And no matter what we had to endure during this era
I fell in love with you more and more by the instant
As we look back year after year with sobbing eyes
You have given me more than a woman can ever imagine
And I truly enjoyed this magnificent ride with you
As we continue to strive for many more adoring years
To share hand-in-hand and arm-in-arm forever
Happy Valentine's Day my love and best friend!

Happy Valentine's Day Mark Cimabue
Loving you everlastingly from Andrea

Happy 40ᵗʰ Anniversary

Forty years ago, we stood in front of God and confessed our love
As the years passed by we survived the madness of this world
But look at us now as we walked through the lion's den together
And sailed the treacherous seas hand-in-hand until we found land
As we watched over one another until we reached this point
Only God can forgive us for our faults we shared together
Because he made us grow younger and younger over the years
And the trails we blazed together was amazingly exquisite
Just being by each other's side for forty years is irreplaceable
And our heart and souls will forever be intertwined as one
Our lives have outshined any story that can ever be written
I see the twinkle in your eyes like you revealed forty years ago
And that sparkle shines bright even to this phenomenal day

Happy 40ᵗʰ Wedding Anniversary
Mr. & Mrs. DeBright

Happy Birthday Dad 2019

I look at what we have discovered over the years
As father and son, and my eyes begin to tear
Because I feel that God made me funny like you
And made me care with a big heart like you
Made half of me to be in the mold of you
As I sit here with my mind all over the place
I pray that you enjoy this year better than the last
And maybe someday you will be proud of me
Just as proud as I am of you being in my life
I pray that today brings many blessings for you
As I wish you a Happy Birthday Dad!

Love you beyond my wildest dreams Dad

Happy Birthday Vickie

In honor of you on this special day in your life
I want to say thank you for accepting me
And making me feel like a part of your family
God has blessed you with another glorious day
To cherish and celebrate amongst family and friends
Because you are in our thoughts and prayers daily
And on this extraordinary day we honor you
May your day shine bright like a summer's day
And your family showers you with lots of love
As we all sing to you Happy Birthday!!!

Happy Birthday Vickie!
I hope you have a wonderful day!

Happy Mother's Day Auntie 2019

If I could write a #1 documentary lifetime story about you
It would just have a few words that say I love You
Because no money, or any fame can say enough
About you and how much you mean to me in my life
Because God continues to grant me you each year
I may be biased but you're the greatest aunt in the world
For always talking me off of the cliffs to avoid any pain
I have lost count of our conversations about my sorrows
But what I do know is that I am grateful, humble and blessed
Because you always give me hope to weather the storms
And today I honor you for all you have done for me
Happy Mother's Day Auntie!!!

I can't love you enough but I will give it my all
Happy Mother's Day love your Nephew

Happy Mother's Day Grandmom 2019

Grandma, On Mother's Day I am reminded that I have not one, but two incredible women role models in my life. Today I celebrate you! Happy Mother's Day

How does a grandmother's love live on inside my heart?
Let me tell you the story of my hearts vision of her love
It begins with how strong willed she was as I grew up
I never ever saw her shed a tear in front of me
And I thought she was superwoman without the cape
My whole life around her I felt safer than a bank vault
Because she was made of the strongest diamond in the world
And as I write this I smile and tear up at the same time
Because my love for her runs deeper than the deepest oceans
So, before I go on and on and begin to ramble
I just want to say Thank You for everything mom
Happy Mother's Day!!!!

Love you beyond the stars My Superwoman
Happy Mother's Day love your Grandson

Happy Mother's Day Mom 2019

Thank you, God, for another year to celebrate this day
Because today this represents a blessing for me
And it gives me goosebumps to say I Love you today mom
Because you have raised me to be respectful to women
Thank you for putting up with me for 48 years
And I pray we get to worship many more special moments
Because we are not promised tomorrow or beyond
But for now, I will store these memories away in my mind
As we take another Mother's Day to share together
I hope you have a fabulously wonderful day mom
Happy Mother's Day Mom!!!!

Love you beyond words can express
Happy Mother's Day love your Son

Happy Mother's Day to all Moms

To all mom's here today and in heaven I thank you
For helping to groom us from infants, kids, teenagers to adults
I would like to take great delight to celebrate you
Because dads are special, but moms are invincible
A mom's love is never ending and their hearts are unbreakable
Honoring moms today is a bonus as we should honor them daily
And I am thankful to all of the women in my life everyday
Because I know each of you has taught me something valuable
Just know that you all have a special place in my heart
And if I don't say it enough God bless each one of you
On allowing me to share another Mother's Day with you
From my heart to you Happy Mother's Day to all Moms today!

Sending blessings & lots of Hugs to all Moms!

Happy Valentine's Day Ladylove

And with each passing year we share a kiss or two
As we snuggle up together and hold each other near
In honor of Valentine's Day celebrated with a cheer
As I look across the dinner table and wink at you my dear
Because on this special day we share another year
With wine, good food and lots of our favorite beer
You are my ladylove that I will cherish like a career
As we celebrate on Valentine's Day this year!

Happy Valentine's Day my Ladylove
Loving you always more and more each year!

Happy Valentine's Day My Love

As we share another year together on Valentine's Day
I look back over the years and realize your still here
And that makes this day more special than any so far
Because we are sharing the most loved crazed day of the year
With each other once again and that hypnotizes my soul
Because a lifetime without you just wouldn't be the same
And the joy that you bring to me makes my world complete
Because my love for you keeps me going each and everyday
As we exchange our thoughts and feelings on this day
I just want to say Happy Valentine's Day My Love!

                                  Happy Valentine's Day My Love
                        Loving you always and forever and ever!

Holiday Love

The weather is changing outside for December
All of the leaves have fallen off the trees
Because Jack Frost is beginning to come alive
The winter air is causing my body to chill
Because the holiday season has arrived
As fond memories of you waltz through my mind
Because I am missing you dearly my love
It never fails during this time of year
Because losing you demolished my soul
With every year, it gets harder to consume
Because what we shared, the most was our love
Just when we had it all it came crashing down
Because you were my Holiday Love

When we first met, it was on my 27th birthday
I remember it just like it was yesterday
Because as I was celebrating with friends
You crossed my path and caught my eye
And for that split-second time stood still
Because you imprisoned my inner foundation
As I turned to watch you walk away
And from that moment I knew you were the one
Because as you walked back toward me
You began to smile and play with your hair
As you got closer you stopped to say hi
And wish me a Happy Birthday and give me a hug
At that moment, I wanted you to be my Holiday Love

Merry Christmas and Happy New Year

2018 is ending with many recollections
As I look deep into my minds memory bank
And scan through the database of memories
That we shared tears, love and laughter
With each other throughout this year
I personally thank God for each of you
Because our family bond is God's blessing
Which is held together with his overwhelming love
And this year may have been tough on us
As God weathered the storm right by our side
And when this year ends we can count our blessings
Whether it was good or bad we made it together
And no matter how 2019 begins for each of us
I know that my Heavenly Father has blessed me
To walk this path with each of you for another year
Merry Christmas and Happy New Year!!!!

Blessing to You on Christmas Day

As I look back upon my life again this year for the holidays
I thank you for putting up with me for 48 years and counting
Because I know that I was not the most behaved kid
And I caused you many restless days and nights in life
But I hope you accept my apology for all those moments
Because I know deep down you love me in many ways
And I hope I can make you proud of me without question
Because you saved my life in ways you cannot imagine
And I am sincerely and undeniably grateful for your love
Tough lessons you taught me are still very hard to learn
And I am thankful to share another holiday with you
This is my blessing to you on Christmas Day!

Chapter 5

INSPIRATIONS

Annamarie Nancy Borden

All my life you have always been my angel
You have made my world complete with your love
That made me grow into the woman I am
And God has blessed me with you from head to toe
As no words can express what my heart feels inside
Because I am truly grateful for my blessing that is you
As you are my shining star that twinkles day & night
Because my soul tingles with every thought of you
And the love we share is like nothing in this world
Because when you look deep into my eyes, they cry love
For the woman that makes my universe come alive with joy
And if I have not told you enough before now I Love You
Because you are the heartbeat deep within my soul
As I stand before you with tears of love in my eyes
Because I am the proudest daughter to ever live
And you mean everything in this world to me
Just so, you know I will always be your biggest fan
Because as a mom your love cannot ever be matched
And your grandkids have the greatest grandmother
As we count our blessing for you each and everyday
I will love you always and forever Annamarie Nancy Borden
Because we will always be "Best Friends" for life

"From your Loving Daughter Lori"

Cast Another Note Commits Energy Revitalization

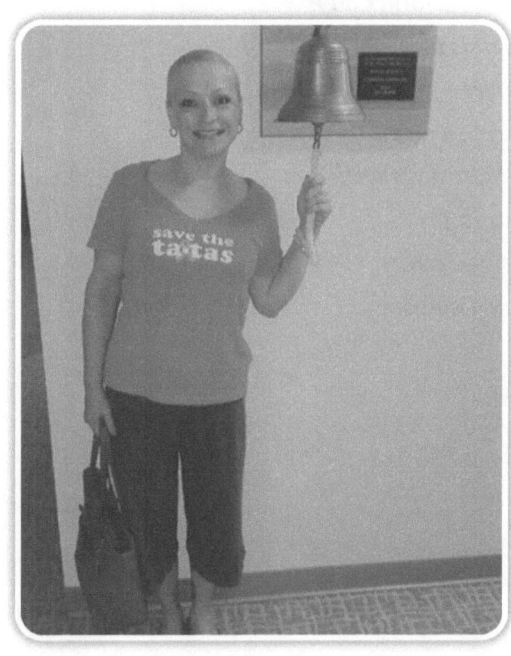

I have a new meaning for the word cancer
And today I am here by your side Ms. Hammond
My friend, my sister and my family
Because this is a battle that will be won
Down in the trenches until the end
And when the dust settles we will be victorious
Because your life matters to each one of us
And like you said cancer picked the wrong b@#$%
Not knowing that you are not the one to mess with
Because we are going to Finish the Fight together
And the game plan on its intentions are misrepresenting
As we change the name in our favor indefinitely to
Cast Another Note Commits Energy Revitalization

Get Well Soon Debbie!

Anything we go through can always be overcome
And I know you had a serious scare the other day
You also gave your family and friends anxiety
As we all gathered together in prayer
Making sure that your soul heard our voice
As God blessed us to share many more days with you
So, before I break down in tears with joy
I want you to know that we love you today
And we want you to get well soon Debbie!

Greatest Masterpiece

I worked with you for many years until last Tuesday
In all our days would I have thought it would be our last?
When I heard the news, I felt a break in my heart
And a big part of my soul had been ripped away
Because not just a friend but a major part of my family
Was just gone with the blink of an eye like a bad storm
I am holding back my emotions on God's behalf right now
Because he put you in my life to keep me humble and strong
And if our paths never cross ever again in the future
I want you to know I will miss you dearly Ms. Colleen Blake
Because you will be remembered in my heart and soul
As part of my life's greatest masterpiece!

H.A.I.L.E.E.

I know you're feeling like the world is crumbling around you
But, God has his arms wrapped around you with love
Even though your emotions are running wild inside
Just take time to sit and talk to our Heavenly Father
And put all your worries, fears and pain in his hands
So, nothing this world can throw at you can break his bond
Because you will always have him standing by your side
He sees your suffering and emotional distress in your heart
All he is waiting for is you to release it upon his plate
God will never leave you or forsake you in your time of need
He hears the tears of your soul calling out to him
So, let him in and watch his healing powers go to work
Remember he loves you for being a child of Christ
Heaven Always Ignites Loves Effort Endlessly

Heaven's Light

Angels come in all forms of life that we admire
Nothing can ever match the blessing of my angel
Because she is the strongest angel of them all
And I thank God for her daily because I love her
As she helped me grow from a boy to a man
With her tough love and amazing heart of gold
Because she has left her imprints on my soul
And God has blessed me to be her grandson
Every day is a blessing to have her in my life
Because my heart beats in unison with hers
And God keeps our love stronger than diamonds
Because you are my Heaven's Light!

Happy Birthday Grandmom!
Love you always and forever your Grandson!

Heaven's Warmth

I pray God continues to lift your soul up with healing
Because Mom you have shown me what family is
And I am beyond grateful for your love and care
Thank you for accepting me as your other son
And always being there for me in every way possible
As I continue to send you my thoughts and prayers
While you begin to heal from all of this pain
I know God has our entire family covered with prayer
Because he is working his healing magic on you
Prayer is the blessing of Heaven's Warmth

Sending you my thoughts and prayers
God Bless You and Get Well Soon Mom!

L.E.S.T.E.R.

We live in a world that has so much pain
And we continue to lose precious lives
Over senseless violence and lack of respect
We have to make a stand and keep the faith
With our kids, neighbors, friends and family
And not give in to the devil's sinful plan to overtake this nation
Because we as people are better than this
And working together we can be One Nation Under God again
Just like we built this land upon over the decades
Let prayer back into our schools for the security of our souls
Give back the power to our parents to direct our kids
As we show the devil we can fill our hearts with love
And make a wonderful world for our leaders of the future
This is called Loves Everlasting Secret To Every Race

L.I.F.E (Love in Faith Everyday)

Hey mom we are here to see you through tough times
And with every obstacle we encounter we will overcome
As God will see us through this moment in time
While he strengthens our souls with everlasting love
Because his magical touch will give you joy in your heart
As he lifts your pain away from your body
So your smiling face can brighten our rooms again
Because each and every day our love for you is never-ending
As we continue to believe in Love in Faith Everyday

God Bless you Mom
My thoughts and prayers go out to you and the family!

Love Joy

Life has many trials and tribulations to overcome
With times of happiness, pain and sorrow
Just as all my days seemed to be lost & over
You came along and rekindled the spark to my heart
Because not only have you loved me for me
But you have rejuvenated my soul like never before
Your love and devotion to me means the world to me
And with each passing day your love enhances my love
Because without you in my life I was lost in this world
However you pulled me from the depths of hell
And into your arms that God made my heaven
With each passing day I Thank You Lord
Not just for bringing this love of mine to me
But because of your undeniable forgiveness and love
For me to be able to live again for years to come
Because you have given me my life back
And to share it with my one and only Love Joy!

Congratulations to Ray Woods & Audrey Woods

M.O.M.

I remember you watching me grow on the streets of the city
And even when I got out of line you set me straight
As a child I didn't understand those little things in life
That would become great lessons to me as I became an adult
Without a doubt you taught me so many values about family
And I could not have made the transition to adulthood
Without you always being caring, loving and an angel
That accepted me as your own even though I was not
But today I cherish you for an eternity forever and ever
Because you are truly a gift from God in my life
And I am truly grateful, humbled and blessed
Thank you My Other Mother (M.O.M)

I love you beyond the farthest galaxy!
Your son from another mother!

Mates of the Soul Forever

Our paths have never been so scripted by God than today
Because today tears will be shed and spirits will fly high
And all God's angels will share our marriage with us
Just knowing that our love for each other will never end
Because the love we share burns deep within our souls
And nothing out of this world can put that fire out
As today we say I do, and begin this journey as one
With foothills to climb and roads to travel beyond the stars
We will forever be known as king and queen today
Because God has joined us together as Mates of the Soul Forever

Congratulations to Mr. and Mrs. Dave Fisher
God Bless You until the End of Time!
Love you both!

Memories of a Lifetime

As your smiles have made a home in my soul
And even with you moving many miles away
I can say that you have gained a friend in me
And remember that is a friend to the end
As dear friends chisel memories in hearts
And you both have etched memories for me
Because you both will be missed sincerely
And I just want to say thanks to you both
For being a part of my life over the years
And making me feel like part of the family
I pray that you both grow young together
As God spreads his blessings upon you
And many incredible memories of a lifetime!

God Bless you Lydia & Ben
You will be missed!

My Letter to God

Heavenly Father, you are the glue that holds together my heart
As I praise your word in my daily life each and every day
And the faith of your word helps ease my mind, body and soul
As I kneel down each night before bed to pray to you Father
And you open your arms and hold me close to your heart
As you whisper to me and send warmth through my flesh
Because you are the alpha and omega that controls my world
And you will never leave me or forsake me
Because I am blessed to be in your presence
As you fill my life with your love and promises
Heavenly Father, thank you for accepting me as your child
And for providing me with the love of praise and faith
As I thank you for the love you give me Father! Amen!

My Sister

I never know when my life is going to turn upside down
However, when it does I have been blessed with love
As that love extends around the world and back
Because when my spirit is feeling low inside
I have the most loving and wonderful human being
To calm my nerves and give her support like no other
She knows just the right formula to soothe my soul
As she bestows my confidence like when I was 9 yrs. old
And not let the agonizing pain overrun my thoughts
As she picks me up when I continue to fall down
Because she is My Sister

When I kneel down at night and pray to the heavens
I know that God has given me that special sister
That knows when to call to make sure I am ok
And provides me hugs when I need them the most
Along with a shoulder to lay on to catch my tears
Because her warm heart comforts & soothes the soul
And with all of the love she has built inside of her
Makes you just want to hold her and never let go
Because she has the power to make your pain go away
As she is a wonderful blessing to have in my life
Because each passing day for me can be a battle
That tests my manhood and free will to survive
However, having her in my corner gives me a fighting chance
Because God allows her to just be My Sister

Poem to the Parents

I know your heart is crying for me
And my spirit and smile is still alive
Because God has called me home
As my pain and suffering is gone
Please dry your eyes from sad tears
And let my spirit comfort your soul
Because I need you to be strong
As my spirit will help you move on
I will always be felt inside your heart

As my love & voice echos through your mind
Take this time to grieve my loss
But don't let your sorrow consume you
Because God is holding me tight
With his comforting arms
As he says to me everything is ok
Because he knows our pain & sorrow
And promises me he will see you through
As I believe in my heart his word is true
I want you to know that I will always love you!

Rose

Life has many obstacles to overcome to be happy
And watching you two over the years is a joy
Because it took you both to get through the thorns
To find each other to help heal the wounds
That you both had to endure to find your perfect rose
To make your lives shine again with the sun
And now that the cloud has passed you by
Your hearts have come into bud just like a rose
I am happy to see you both bask in each other's happiness
Because that just makes your love nurture in this world
And it continues to help with the flourishing of your rose

God Bless you Jennifer & Dave
Congratulations for finding your Rose!

Sweet Dot

This is my prayer for you my sister
Because I know what you are going through is tough
However, you have us to lean on in your time of need
Because we will not let you go through it alone
And we will stand by your side to overcome this illness
As it may seem to be overwhelming at times
I can truly say that you provide us strength to cope
And we will provide you strength to destroy and conquer
Because you have been tough your whole life
And I refuse to let you hang your head low
Because all things can be vanquished with faith
And as long as God is by your side all things are possible
As I may shed a tear or two for you to get better
Those tears bring me greater faith and belief in God
Because he gave his only son for us to give us life
And each prayer doesn't go unheard
Because our Lord and Savior hears our prayers
And he answers us when we least expect it everyday
Nevertheless, he will hear our prayers for you and heal you
Because you are his and our sweet Dot

I may be a complete stranger to you with this poem
But believe me God knows that we are not strangers in him
No matter if we never met we are all family
Because we are all God's children
And he has granted me with the power to bless others
Because of his love for us, he gives us hope & faith
And with his blessing for you he is providing me with peace
Because he wants me to pray for you my sister at heart
And I want to pass this prayer to you from my heart
Because you will stand by my side and laugh and smile
With the blessing that God provides you through us
Because you are his and our sweet Dot

Victory

Heaven has many blessings to provide you in your life
And God wants to free you from any dejection
So, he can hold you close in his warm and loving arms
As he lifts up your spirits in prayer each and everyday
Just letting you know he can and will heal all wounds
Because his grace and mercy provides courage and trust
As his angels sing praise upon your soul for comfort
And his faith will shine bright inside your heart
While his gentle touch will run through your veins
To calm your mind, body and soul in victory

Sending you my thoughts and prayers
God Bless You Joan Griffith

World's Greatest Stepson

Today I become an extended part of the family
And by the tears that are gushing down my face
You two became the most important part of my life
And I Thank God, every passing day for this blessing
Because you brought love and tenderness to my heart
And with every ounce of my blood I love you
No stepmom can ever imagine having a perfect stepson
And my heart shouts out deep within my soul with joy
Because I can watch you grow into a great young man
As my spirit will forever be filled with happiness
And that makes my life magnificent and extraordinary
To call you the world's greatest stepson!

Collin Michael Gilbert
Your Stepmom loves you very much!

Chapter 6

AFTER DARK

Black & Sexy

I think of caressing your body with my gentle touch
And slowly kiss you on your neck and on your lips
As I slide my tongue down upon your breast
And open my mouth wide to suck on your nipples
As I cup your juicy butt cheeks in my hands
And squeeze them tight as you arch your back
I gradually remove your clothes from your skin
As I strip down to my birthday suit for you
And look you in your eyes and tell you I love you
As I leisurely move in to give you a passionate kiss
And begin to make love to you for the rest of the night
As we sweat the night away Black & Sexy

Exquisite

What I witnessed last night seeing you was amazing
Just talking with you before seeing you was great
However, I was truly impressed with what I saw
Because you were just as lovely as your voice sounded
Your 5'5 build and green eyes blew my mind
However, there was more to you than meets the eye
Let me start with the tight fit body you possess
The small soft lips that made me want to kiss
With your gorgeous, smile that made my body twitch
Because you are Exquisite

I know you have something going through your mind
I am curious to find out what those thoughts could be
However, I am going to give you my creative thoughts
You look tense so we have to loosen you up
As I would massage your head with my fingers
Then work my way down to your shoulders
As I begin to rub you all over your back to relax you
Then pull your hair back as I kiss you upon your neck
As my soft kisses makes your body quiver
Because you are Exquisite

If my soft kisses don't get you all hot and bothered
Then let me tell you more that will be in store
After your back rub and shoulder massage
I will have you stretch out on the couch
Then remove your shoes and grab the lotion
As I begin to massage your feet from your heels to toes
Then work my way up each leg one by one
As I watch every facial expression, you make
Because you are Exquisite

Now that you have placed your body in my hands
I begin to remove your mini-shirt and sweater
As you are laying there in just your underwear
Because you have lost yourself in the moment
As I lean down to kiss you on your navel
And feel your inside muscles tighten up
As you run your hands down my back
Because with my every touch you lose control
Now my motivation is to get you ready for excitement
Because you are Exquisite

As I reach over to grab the ice cubes for us
I begin to rub them up and down your body
As your body approaches the pinnacle of bliss
You slowly raise your legs as your toes curl
Because now your body wants satisfaction
However, it is not the time just yet for you
Because I still have more exploring to do
As my tongue has to study you from top to bottom
Because the handling of ice has just begun
As I work my way down to your feet
Because you are Exquisite

I have reached my starting point on your body
As I place the ice cubes inside of my mouth
Then I slowly place each toe inside my mouth
As I roll your toes and the ice around with my tongue
And watch your eyes roll back inside your head
Because you are encountering a unique feeling
As you, dig your nails into the couch pillows
And begin to breathe heavier with each stroke
As your body is thirsting for more pleasure
Because you are Exquisite

Head to Toe

The night is here and the mood is right
Because my baby is coming over for dinner
And I have a long night planned for her
As I finish getting the table set
And I begin to light the candles
As I check the final stages of dinner
I head into the room to get dressed
Because I can't wait to see my lady
And hold her extremely close in my arms
As I watch her walk from head to toe

As the doorbell rings, I go open the door
And standing there is my love with that sexy smile
Looking tantalizing and sweet as honey dew
And my eyes light up from all of her beauty
As my jaw begins to drag along the floor
Because you are looking so exquisite
In that tight fitting, black body dress
All I can do is watch you walk
And imagine kissing you from head to toe

As I grab our dinner entrees to sit down
You walk up behind me to rub my back
As I turn around you blow me a kiss
Because you can't believe your eyes
As I pour you a glass of chardonnay
And give you a kiss before you sit down
Because this special night has just begun
And I have a full agenda for my love
As I can't wait to love you from head to toe

As we make it back to the couch
I pull you close from behind
And start to kiss you on your neck
As you, tell me to unzip your dress
I waste no time to grant your wish
As the zipper, moves slowly down your back
Just as your dress falls to the floor
You show off your fabulous sexy lingerie
And it is one of my favorite colors Red
As I'm ready to love you from head to toe

Hug & Kiss

Laying there with that soft vanilla skin from head to toe
Can drive any man wild and make your mouth water
Because when you sent me the latest picture of you
I couldn't stop thinking about licking you all over
Because looking at you brought back memories
As I shake my head to escape my extravagant thoughts
That cruise through my mind when I envision you
As I try to focus very hard on the matter at hand
Which is your birthday today that you are celebrating?
I want to send my personal birthday wishes to you
As you have etched yourself into my mind, body and soul
Because I can't wait to see you again face to face
So, I can see that lovely smile and those sweet lips
As I sneak you a special hug and kiss

I Can't Get Enough of You

Seeing you looking so beautiful last night
It made my feelings become more intense
As I became more aroused than ever before
I wanted to scoop you up off your feet
As I hold you and kiss you for hours
And then begin to lick you all over your body
As I remove your shirt and bra
And begin to gently caress your breast
As I work my tongue toward your belly button
Because I can't get enough of you

Even though we are apart, I still notice you
Like the fresh pedicure on your feet
And looking at them just drove me wild
As it does when you touch me
And you put your feet in front of me
I just cannot seem to control myself
Because as we make love and your feet touch me
I lose all control and it turns me on
Because I can't get enough of you

*I miss all of the cuddling, touching & kissing
And I want to work on getting that back
Because you're all I ever wanted
And I want to show you every single day
Because my heart is lost without you
And I know it is going to take you time
But all I can say is I can wait
Because you are, everything in this world to me
And I will make it worth your while
Every day you allow me to show you
Because it's you that I want in my life
And I love you more than words can express
Because I can't get enough of you*

Latin Lover

As I watch, you walk across the parking lot
And head up to the room in your black pumps
I had to sit down before I collapse to the floor
Because seeing your beauty made my knees quiver
As you begin to move closer to the room
My mind begins to lose all control of its thoughts
And the spine-tingling sensation that I feel inside
Is driving me wild with deep lust for you
Because as you walk through the door
I just melt in my chair as you call my name
Because you are my Latin Lover

As I stare deep into your sexy Latin eyes
I hear your body crying out to my soul
As I reach out to grab your hand
And pull you close into my arms
As my hands begin to caress your curves
While our body temperatures begin to rise
And our hearts begin to beat as one
As I begin to kiss you all over your body
And you begin to moan and call me papi
Because you are my Latin Lover

As you jump into my arms as we fall onto the bed
I begin to work my way down to remove your skirt
As you arch your back as I kiss you upon your neck
And I begin to lick you upon your thighs
Just to here you call out my name
And begin to dig your nails into my back
As I place ice in my mouth
And begin to escort it all over your body
From head to toe until your body gets the chills
As you start to bite down on your bottom lip
And your hormones start to rage out of control
Because you're my Latin Lover

Long-Distance Love Affair

As I lay on my side under the warm covers
And listen to the waves crash upon the beach
While the scent of the fresh water warms my soul
Because all I can think of is you holding me tight
As you kiss me tenderly upon the back of my neck
And your soft lips cause chills up and down my spine
That propels my heart into the depths of outer space
Because your gentle stroke upon my juicy thighs
Makes me claw my nails deep into the satin sheets
As the fluids begin to overfill my kitty Kat
And I can't control the throbbing all over my body
Just as I turn over to look you in your eyes
I think of our long-distance love affair

As you lay your finger over my lips to quite my moans
And begin to run your fingers through my hair
As you leisurely work your tongue down my body
Because what I'm experiencing is blowing my mind
And the intensity in my soul is burning with anticipation
As the pulsation of my organs are raging through my skin
Because just knowing what's in store has me yearning for you
As this passionate night is days in the making
And my body has reached the brink of no return
Because you take my breath away with every stroke
As this is how you wrap up our long-distance love affair

Oh My!

How is it I become all hot & bothered thinking about you?
It accelerates my passion for you from head to toe
Because it makes my body tremble all over
Just the thought of your presence drives me crazy
As I want to caress your smooth silky skin
And rub you all over in all the right places
Because all I can say is oh my!

Passion is a strange and beautiful thing to me
Because my passion goes through the roof
As I can make you fall deep into the mood
Just let me tell you what I can make you do
As I begin to kiss you all over your neck
You start to arch your back repeatedly
As your toes curl inside your heels
And the soothing feeling is mesmerizing
As your eyes start to roll back in your head
Because all you can whisper is oh my!

Your heartbeat is racing through your body
As if it wants to spring out of your skin
Because what's going on with you is exciting
And both sets of your lips start to drip
However, I have only just begun your voyage
As I will make you lose total control
While you get wetter and wetter deep inside
As you lock your legs around my waist
And the look of love on your face
Makes me say, oh my!

On the Horizon

Letting you go is not that easy to do
Because I can't shake you from my mind
As my days turn to night, I want you
Because my haunted fantasies have come true
And you appear in all of my current dreams
As the love interest that I want more and more
To caress your pretty hot and tempting body
As I raise you up into my arms off the floor
And slowly walk you over to the sunroom
As I kiss your sweet succulent lips
While I lay you down upon the assorted pillows
As you stare out on the horizon

This moment in time is so precious to our minds
That we captivate our souls in the glare of the moon
Because in an instant we begin to fall deep in love
As you whisper, I love you repeatedly in my ear
And you slowly shake your head in consent
As you tell me, you are ready for me to make love to you
Because our fantasy has come true and became a reality
And it has you tingling in places like never before
Because your stimulation has you on the verge of eruption
As our bodies create such a heat wave pressed together
While we steam up the glass on the horizon

As I remove your clothes with one clean sweep of my hands
Because we both can't withstand each other's touch
As I lightly fondle your inner thighs with my kisses
You begin to whimper as you tense up your legs
And your hormones kick into overdrive with eagerness
As I transfer my body into position with assurance
And our passion cannot wait any longer to explore
Because this will be our very first time with each other
And the feeling of this moment is out of this world
As I start to make love to you on the horizon

As the passion begins to intensify between us
I leisurely lick you from one breast to the other
As you lean up and gently bite me upon my neck
And you dig your nails into my lower back to hold on tight
Because I have your body going into constant spasms
As my long drawn out strokes keep you guessing
Because you haven't felt this way in a long time
As you are being cherished by your lover this way
And it has your emotions in a disorderly state
As our bodies shine on the horizon

One in a Million

As we sit down for our candlelight dinner by the bay
You stand up and excuse yourself for the powder room
As I watch you walk away, you turn back and smile
At that very moment, a warm feeling overtakes my body
As I grab a quick drink of water to cool my soul
Just waiting to see you walk back to the table
Therefore, I can stand and pull out the chair for you
As you slowly settle back into your chair for dinner
Because as I stare at you I feel like one in a million

I look at you and my mind spins around and around
It is as if I am on a circus ride when I am near you
I cannot explain the feelings that run through my soul
Because it makes my body weak and my knees buckle
All I can do to stop this spinning is to hold on tight
Because the things you make me feel is one in a million

I have turned you onto something fun and unique
Because when I used ice on your toes for the first time
It made you experience something you never felt before
Because you could never imagine the treat that was in store
All I know is with every picture or thought of your feet
It turns me on to the point I just do not want to stop
Because what I feel is one in a million

S. L. (Stimulating Love)

I cannot shake these feelings that are in my head
But by having these feelings I want you more and more
We both cannot fight the temptations that we have inside
That is why you are my S.L.

You can only imagine what is in store
However, what is in store will have you asking for more
Starting with your sexy lips
As I work my way down to your sexy toes
Where I may end up only our hearts will know
That is why you are my S.L.

I know you want me to chill but your beauty keeps me going
As your smile turns my grey skies blue
When I am around you, I cannot control my feelings
Nevertheless, I do know one thing it's all good
That is why you are my S.L.

I think I will end here and let your mind fill in the rest
But don't worry it's worth every thought
As it feels right in my heart, how I feel for you
Because I have never felt this way about anyone
That is all I will say right now on paper
That is why you are my S.L.

Sea Blue Dress

We are thousands of miles apart from each other
And I cannot stop looking at your pictures in my mind
Because your smile makes my fire burn inside
As I imagine sweeping you off your feet into my arms
And carry you over to the couch as I whisper in your ear
Because I want you to fall head over heels for me
And make this moment a special one that you will not forget
As I slowly lay you along the cushions on the couch
I hear the pitter-patter of your heart beating against my skin
As you run your tongue across the back of my neck
And make my eyes close with the blink of an eye
Because at that moment my heart stood still
And my breath was taken away with every soft stroke
As I see you laying there in your Sea Blue Dress

I reach, up and pull your hair back out of your face
As you let out a silent sigh as you grip my hands
And you slowly shake your head repeatedly
As you stare into my eyes as you bite your lip
Because you are enjoying how I am making you feel
And the way you are feeling is so gratifying
As you move in close to grab my face with both hands
And you moisten your lips to give me a big kiss
Because you know your kisses soothe my soul
As I fall deep into the gentleness of your touch
Because of how you make me lose control of myself
As I plunge into your arms just like a little kid
Because I just want to be close to you forever right now
As I snuggle into the couch with you in my arms
I cannot help but to stare at you in your Sea Blue Dress

As you take my hands and run them along your thighs
Because you want me to touch you all over your body
Nevertheless, you want me to take my time and do it right
Because you want me to take you to the point of no return
As you slip into the brink of going wild from within
Because with every passing stroke you arch your back
As you call out my name with strong conviction
Because I am sending your mind into a momentary tailspin
As you lift your left leg up over the back of the couch
And quickly remove your shoes from your feet
Because you know how your feet drives me wild
As you begin to rub them along my legs
Until I cup my hands underneath your hips
As I kiss, you up and down along your neck
Because I love you in your Sea Blue Dress

As you lay motionless on the couch with your body trembling
I get up to open the curtains and turn out the lights
As I turn and watch the moonlight shine upon your face
And the twinkle in your eyes percolates with passion
As you begin to tease me by pointing your legs in the air
Then you reach up and rub your hands all over your body
Until you stop your hands upon your breast
And that stops me in my tracks for a minute
As I stumbled back over to the chair with a smile
Because all I can think about now is making love to you
As you have set the foreplay mode into overdrive
With your hot and heavy antics within my mind
And I cannot get you out of my thoughts
Because I love seeing you in that Sea Blue Dress

Spoken Words

Kisses can make your body tingle
Hugs can make you safe and warm
However, passion can blow your mind
And making love will drive you wild
As you imagine all of these spoken words

As I suck on your painted toes with ice
And wander my tongue up your thighs
As you take deep, uncontrollable breathes
Because your body control begins to weaken
With every passing stroke, up and down your body
And the only thing you can think about is sex
Because your mind has been introduced to the spoken words

Just as you, begin to rub your hands over your breast
And your eyes start to roll back into your head
As I passionately kiss you along your waistline
With my soft lips until you let out a loud, moan
As your body shakes profusely inside my arms
Because your concentration has you excited
With the thoughts of love making all night
Because ringing in your head are these spoken words

As we allow our passion to simulate what comes next
You vibrate a sigh that only means one thing for you
And that is take me right now because I'm yours
As you hurry to remove the remains of your clothes
Just as I hit the power button to turn on some slow jams
You reach up and pull my shirt over my head
And pull me in close to suck on my nipples
As you, roll your tongue over them repeatedly
I start to call out your name uncontrollably
Because this is the passion of the spoken words

Chapter 7

MEMOIRES

Eyes of a Woman

It is getting closer for me to start vacation
As I prepare to wrap up here at work
Just as I start to shut down for the night
My phone rings and it's my best friend Maria
As I pick up the phone, she tells me about a trip
That she and some other women have planned
To go away for a girl's week long retreat
However, I could use the getaway for me
Therefore, I decided to accept the proposal
As I gather my things to get ready
And look out upon the afternoon sky
As I gaze through the Eyes of a Woman

Maria pulls up to pick me up for the trip
As we load up my things in the van
She looks over to me with concern
And she begins to walk toward me
Because she knows what I must be feeling inside
She begins to proceed to give me a hug
Because she wants me to release my pain
While I try to enjoy my time away from home
Because she sees the sadness on my face
As she gazes through the Eyes of a Woman

As we head over to pick up the ladies
I reach over and thank her for the invite
As she says you're welcome softly to me
She promises to keep everything hush, hush
I turn away to look out the window
As my eyes, begin to welt up with tears
Because I want to be in my ex-boyfriends arms

Nevertheless, I know that it is not possible
Because he made a mistake in our relationship
And right now, I cannot shake it out of my mind
Even though we are separated, I still think of him always
Because my love is still strong for him inside
As I stare through the Eyes of a Woman

We arrive to pick up the rest of the ladies
As they approach the car, my temperature rises
Because it is her that interfered with my relationship
And my mouth dropped to the ground
I reached over to Maria and said I cannot go
As she asked me why and pulled me to the side
I could not control myself to get the words out
However, she knew right then that this would be hard
As we continued to walk over to the trees
She finally got me to calm down to tell her
That's the woman Sadie who broke up my relationship
Even though nothing even happened between them
I just could not take the pain that I felt inside
As I express myself through the Eyes of a Woman

Maria told me to have faith in her and God
And they both will get me through this time away
Because she wanted me to go and open up my soul
Therefore, God can work on healing my trauma inside
I agreed to go as long as she promised to keep Sadie away
And she crossed her heart and said my wish is your command
Because she knew that until I faced my pain
I would never get the strength to move forward
Because Maria knew me oh so well inside & out
She always had my best interest at heart
Because she gazed through the Eyes of a Woman

As we began to head out on our road trip
I closed my eyes and all I could see is my love
As I drifted, off to sleep with him on my mind
I started to reminisce of the times we shared
As he would hold me, close in his arms
Tell me how beautiful I looked no matter what
As I felt safe when he was ever so close
Because I knew, he meant every word
And I would always be special in his heart
Because he made me feel like no other could make me feel
I knew he treated me as if I was the only one in this world
As I woke up from my dream with a smile on my face
Because I dreamed through the Eyes of a Woman

Maria yelled ladies we have arrived to our destination
As we pulled up to the secluded home in the mountains
We all were like in shock to see the beauty of the home
Because we had never seen anything like it in our lives
But as we gathered our things to head inside
As I stood there on the porch taking pictures
Maria placed her arm around me with joy
And told me you can open up and be free
Because she promised me that this trip will be good for me
And that Mother Nature would soothe my soul
Just as long as I placed my worries in God's hands
Because he would help me release the pain
As I seen the vision through the Eyes of a Woman

As the moonlight shined bright in the sky
And the stars shined ever so beautiful
I grabbed my jacket to take a walk along the path
Because I needed to be alone to think and pray
As I walked along the path I began to speak to God
And I asked him why do I feel so sad inside

Because I can't get over the love of my life
And I know that if we could get what we had back
Things would have to change for us to survive
And I would take that chance to be together again
However, we would need to start over slow & new
Because I want him in my life
As the tears ran down my face
From the Eyes of a Woman

As I stare off into the moon-lit sky
I felt the cool breeze blow upon my face
And my body began to shiver inside
As I headed back to the beautiful home
I hear Maria calling my name along the path
As I get closer she meets me half way with a smile
And she runs up to give me a hug like a child
As I look into her eyes and they are glowing
She tells me to close my eyes for a big surprise
As I kept them closed until we reached the house
I hear the voices of the women on the porch
I ask Maria can I open my eyes she says not yet
Because she is looking through the Eyes of a Woman

To make sure I do not look she covers my eyes
And the cool breeze blows through the trees
However, the scent that comes my way smells familiar
As I try to remember the smell
Maria removes her hands from my eyes
As I open my eyes standing there is my ex
I am in total shock to see him here
As I turn to Maria she said it was not me
Because she didn't bring her cell phone
And the only phone was down the road at the store
Because it was supposed to be a women's only trip
As I stared through the Eyes of a Woman

My eyes began to welt up with tears
As he approached me I thanked God for this chance
To make it right between the both of us
He reached out to me with open arms
As I saw the tears running wildly down his face
I knew he came to fight for the love he had for me
As he stuttered his words in between his tears
He told me he was sorry for the pain he had caused
And I felt the sincerity from his heart & soul
Because I knew God had answered my prayers
And wanted to let me know that he holds me in his hands
Because he always sees through the Eyes of a Woman

As we walked along the path hand-in-hand
He pulled me close to keep me warm
And I felt like the luckiest girl in the world
Because he came all this way for me
As we reached the edge of the trees
That looked out over the hillside
As he turned to face me and look me in my eyes
He yelled out over the mountaintop to tell the world
That he loved me and would never ever let me go
As he dropped to one knee to confess his love to me
His tears began to run constantly upon his face
As he looked up at me in the moonlight
I see the thoughts of him losing me were real
Because that is what I see through the Eyes of a Woman

As he rose up to his feet with sadness on his face
I pulled him into my arms and just held him tight
Because I felt more love for him than I ever felt
And it made my soul glow brighter than the stars
Because I knew this was my true love standing here
And I did not want to let him go for anything

As our hearts were beating against each other's inside
I leaned back to look upon his face
And I moved in close to give him a kiss
Because I needed to feel his soft lips touching mine
As I felt the fireworks go off inside of me
With the soft touch of his lips caressing mine
As this is what I have been missing for sometime
Because I love what I see through the Eyes of a Woman

I know our journey will be tough to overcome
Nevertheless, he has always been there for me
More than anyone in all of my other relationships combined
I have never been treated as great as he has treated me
Because deep down I know I love him deeply
And I know he still loves me just the same
However, I want to take it slow and I need to know
If that is something he is willing to do for us
Because I miss him completely being in my life
As he makes me feel so warm and fuzzy inside
When he holds me in his arms I know I am home
Because I see him through the Eyes of a Woman

As he escorts me back down to the house
And we arrive to the porch to say goodbye
He drops to his knees and thanks God for this moment
Because he confesses his heart & soul to God
While he is kneeling in front of me in person
Because he relinquishes his flesh to God & me
And he stands up to kiss my hand to head home
As he turns to walk to his car I tell him to wait
Because I tell him I am willing to work on us
However, I still need to take this time away for me
As he says to me that he will wait for an eternity
And walk to the ends of the earth to make me his again

He walks over to me for the last time to give me a kiss
And before he does he looks deep into my soul
Because he wants me to feel his love from within
As he scoops me up off my feet and kisses me
Until I just feel all of my limbs go numb
Because I felt the passion that we still shared
And I understood from that moment that he was the one
Because I felt his love warming me through the Eyes of a Woman

As he carried me up to the front door and put me down
He turned around and headed to his car
As he pulled away and blew me kisses
I caught them and placed them close to my heart
As I entered the beautiful home and closed the door
Standing there next to the fireplace was Maria
And she asked me how it went
However, I did not hear a word she said
Because I was floating on another planet
As she snapped me out of my daze
I looked at her with some disappointment
Because I was kind of upset & happy all rolled into one
As she said what's the matter did he hurt you again
I said no but I told her she should have not invited him here
And she swore to me that she did not tell him
Because she knew that he would have tried to stop her
From coming up here with the women to get peace
Nevertheless, I said if it was not you then who did then
And she asked me did I pray on the relationship
As I thought about it I said to Maria yes
Then she said then there is your answer
And I said how is this my answer to the situation
She said God answered your prayer for you
Because he sees everything through the Eyes of a Woman

As I stood in front of Maria and the fireplace
It dawned on me that if you pray to God
That he will answer your prayers when he knows you need it
And he gave me my answer to what needs to happen for us
Because he sees the lovely bond we shared together
And he is granting us the opportunity to revive it again
Because he sees the true pain we are feeling inside
As we are broken without having each other in our lives
Because we have encountered so much in the time we were together
And no matter what we stood by each other for everything
Because he made me feel like no other woman in this world
Even though I still feel the hurt inside my heart
I truly do love him still deeply within my soul
Because that is what I see through the Eyes of a Woman

As we fall asleep in the chairs talking by the fire
And morning comes earlier than we expected
However, as the birds begin to sing outside on the porch
I stand up and stretch to head outside to get some air
As I open the door to step outside I run into Sadie
And I felt the awkwardness building up between us
Nevertheless, she said could she talk to me very quickly
I wanted to say no but I knew I had to conquer this pain
And she told me that nothing ever happened
Between my ex and her not even a little bit
Just at that moment Maria was standing in the doorway
And as Sadie assured me that nothing happened
Because she knew how much he loved me from within
And she felt more for him but he said he only loved you
Because he told her that every time they ran into each other
And she apologized to me if she made us separate
However, she needed to get that off her chest
Because it was eating at her inside for weeks
And I accepted her apology and Maria smiled

Because I finally took her advice to conquer my pain
As I looked through the Eyes of a Woman

Now that we have cleared the air and moved on
And we have decided to enjoy our last moments here
Because we would have to leave this beautiful place
And head home to our busy working lives again
However, I feel so much better inside than I ever did
And while I finished packing my things
I knelt down and thanked God for saving me
Because he made me learn and grow as a woman
As I now understand that things happen for a reason
And love is a beautiful thing to experience
Because no matter what, if you trust in him you can persevere
And he will give you the strength to overcome the pain
However, at the same time you need to move forward to the future
And not allow your past discretions to stop you from love
Because he knows what to look for through the Eyes of a Woman

As we all say goodbye to the lovely home for the last time
And begin our journey back to the big city life
I take one last mental picture of my time here
Because one day I will come back here
However, it will be for another special occasion I hope
Because this is a place I will cherish forever
As it has created a new chapter in my life
Now it is up to me to continue that chapter
As I thank Maria for bringing me along
I look back at Sadie and tell her thank you
And she has this shocked look on her face
Nevertheless, she slowly says you're welcome
And Maria grabs my hand and shakes her head
Because she knows that I have released all my pain
As we both look through the Eyes of a Woman

Our trip is over and Maria drops me off at home
As she helps me unload my bags from the van
She gives me a big hug with tears in her eyes
And I ask her what's wrong?
She tells me that she also prayed for my relationship
Because she knew that I had a good man
And he would give his life for me
Even though he may have taken it for granted
He always spoke about me every chance he got
Because for every bad thing there were four good things
And he missed me more than I could ever know
However, he made sure that going forward he would change
As the light shined through the Eyes of a Woman

Now that I'm settled back at home in my own bed
I get ready to go to sleep as I say my prayers
And turn out the light I stare at the ceiling
Because all I can think about is my baby confessing his love
As I have tears of joy run down my face
Because he proved a lot to me by showing up
However, what made it even more special was God's work
And I thank him every minute of the day
Because he has brought joy back into my life
And I know what my next steps will be
As I close my eyes and fall into a deep sleep
Because I have seen my vision through the Eyes of a Woman

As the morning came for me to start my day
I reached over to grab the phone and it began to ring
As I said hello Maria said good morning sunshine
And I said good morning back to her
Because I was shocked to hear from her so early
Nevertheless, she told me to get showered and dressed for breakfast
As I hung up the phone to go get in the shower

I could not help but wonder what is going on
However, I just did as she asked without any questions
And I knew Maria was always looking out for me
Because she was like my big sister that I always wanted
And she wanted us to do something with just us
Because I looked through the Eyes of a Woman

As I was in the shower she left me a message to meet at Gavin's Cuisine
I think to myself why Gavin's Cuisine that is a fancy place
To meet for breakfast and she sounded excited
Now I was wondering what good news she had received
As I dug deep into my closet for my finest dress
Because I know this must be some huge news
And I wanted to make my big sister's moment special
Because she would do the same thing for me
As I arrive to Gavin's Cuisine the waiter greeted me
And he said follow me please to the private room
As I enter the room it is filled with candles burning
And the fireplace is burning as well early this morning
I ask the waiter do you know where Maria is
He responded that she would be right back
Because I am looking through the Eyes of a Woman

As I wait for Maria the waiter brings me some water
I check my watch and 15 minutes have passed
And I begin to get worried about Maria
Because she never keeps anyone waiting long
As I hear the door opening up behind me
I see the violinist playing soft music
And right behind him enters Maria & her husband and my ex
I stand up in amazement to see him
And he is dressed in his finest suit I bought for him
As my parents and his parents enter behind him
He walks over to me in front of the fireplace

And begins to tell me a story about us
Because it reminds him of when we first met
And how I made him feel when he gave me that first kiss
As I am looking through the Eyes of a Woman

I cannot believe what is going on here today
As he continues on with his heartfelt story about us
And the violinist plays softly in the back ground
As he reaches out to hold my hands in his hands
My eyes begin to welt up with tears of joy
As our moms and Maria begin to cry with me
He promises me that he will never hurt or leave me again
Because I am his whole world and his twinkling star
And he could not swallow the fact of losing me
As it made him not eat or sleep for days
That is when he felt God touch his soul
To come and fight for my love and forgiveness
And to get another chance at happiness with me
Because he realized the vision through the Eyes of a Woman

My tears began to run down my face like a stream flowing
And he used his hands to wipe them away from my face
As his voice began to tremble in between his tears
Because he was speaking confidently from his heart
And I knew right then that he meant every word
Because I had never seen this in him before
And it made me start crying within my soul

As he continued on to express his love to me
I clutched his hands tighter within mine
Because I knew that I did not want this moment to end
However, I knew that he would close out his story
And I would have to prepare for it ending
Because I could picture this moment through the Eyes of a Woman

Now my baby's tears were flowing like a stream along his face
And it made me realize how sincere his words meant
Because he did not blink not even once during his story
And my legs began to quiver underneath my body
However, just at that moment he dropped to his knees
And he was reaching into his pocket for something
As the ring sparkled from the light of the fire
It was a thing of pure beauty and elegance
As he looked up into my eyes still not blinking
Along with the tears still flowing down his face
He asked me if I would marry him
And he said even if I said no he would wait forever
Because he will travel to the farthest galaxy for me
And I began to cry through the Eyes of a Woman

As our family & friends waited for me to answer
I needed to sit down before I collapsed from the shock
Because this was going to be the biggest decision of my life
As I looked deep into his eyes and said yes, yes, yes
Then my mom began to cry countless tears of joy
As our family & friends rushed over to give us tons of hugs
And my soon-to-be husband held me close in his arms
Because I have been waiting for this special moment
And it has finally come to realization in my life
Because I have found the love I have been missing
And what I'm feeling is bitter sweet to me
Because I just needed to be patient through the Eyes of a Woman

Last Prayer

I have been sitting here not knowing what to do
Because I cannot focus on anything but you
I miss you so much that I am going crazy
However, with all this time, all I do is think of you
And I realize I want you back in my life
Even if it means dropping everything for you
Because I can't seem to shake you from my mind
And my heart is crying out to my soul
Because my heart, my mind and soul wants you back
And my emotions continue to run wild
Just when I think I am ok, I begin to cry
Because this may be my Last Prayer

I never knew that loving you would be this wonderful
Because the moment you came into my life
It made me encounter something more than special
And what I realized is that you were the one
Even though I hurt you deep inside your core
I still want to be the one to erase that pain away
Because with every passing moment I miss you
As I sit here and see your pretty smile
I pray for another chance to be with you
Because this is my Last Prayer

I know that interracial relationships are tense
Whether it is between families or the world
However, what I feel for you is worth the disapproval
Because you are the glue that made me strong
As I went through some tough times in my life
And I know I may not have shown gratitude
Nevertheless, I knew I needed to give you more credit

Because you made me feel wanted again
And I didn't realize it until now
How much you truly mean to me in my heart
Because you helped me love the right way
As we spent our days and nights together
I want you back in my life forever and ever
Because this is my Last Prayer

It has been three months since we have talked
That is because I needed time away from you
Because I knew the pain that, I caused you
And I knew talking to you would break my heart
Because I could hear the pain in your voice daily
And I know you still feel a lot of that pain
However, my love I want to do what I can to erase the pain
If that even means waiting for you forever
Because baby I Love You more and more each day
And it drives me crazy to see your beautiful face
Because I want you back in my life for good
As this is my Last Prayer

I want your friendship back in my life
Then gradually work on becoming us again
And this time I am going to give you the world
Because the time away has helped me figure it out
And I know now that I need you in my life
Because you graced my soul with your love
And with that love I took for granted my dear
I will make this right for us to get what we shared back
As I sit here writing about you I get all warm and fuzzy
Because those are the feeling that you gave me from the start
And I want to feel these feelings with you all over again
Because I can truly say this is my Last Prayer

Love Beyond Love

As time in our lives passed us by
You make it hard to let you go
Because I never felt love like this before
And it makes my soul sprout wings inside
Because you have my heart in your hands
As I can't imagine you not being with me
However, I know that your pain is great within
Because you are holding onto many past issues
And I do know that it can kill our futures
Because I have never learned to let go of the pain
Until I met you because you were more than special
You showed me what it means to love for real
That is what you gave me from within
Because that is Love Beyond Love

When we met for the first time, I felt something special
As the saying goes, it was love at first sight
However, I never believed that old wive's tale
Until I met you and it changed me forever
Looking at your brown skin and those light hazel eyes
And your beauty made me stagger constantly
Because I could not believe, what my eyes were seeing
As you unlocked my love with your soft touch
And right then I knew I had to have you in my life
Because you alone could make me whole again
And I could not resist the temptation of your voice
Because I wanted to experience you next to me
Every morning, noon and night for the rest of my life
As I feel the Love Beyond Love

You can always fall in love with many souls
However, what you brought to the table for my mind
And then my heart and soul was like a dream come true
Because I wanted you to be mine like a fine wine
As you began to talk to me with that sexy voice
I could not shake the jitters I had inside of my body
And the more you talked to me the more nervous I became
However, your gentle touch released me from my trance
As it made me feel like a teenager all over again
Because I began to shrug my shoulders and blush
As you brushed your hands upon my sensitive skin
I felt like I was among the clouds with the angels
Because at that moment I felt the Love Beyond Love

With these half-crazy feelings running through my veins
I realized that you can jump start my tenderness
And provide me with that missing puzzle piece in my soul
Because you have unlocked my hidden treasure
And I am grateful for your patience with me
As we build the trust, time and special moments together
While I keep handing more of my soul over to you
Because you made me the apple of your eyes
And that feeling is like a volcano erupting
Deep within my most inner regions of my soul
And I do not ever want this feeling to go away
As it has helped my mind understand my thirst
And it is the joy of Love Beyond Love

My Boo

As the lightning strikes outside the airport window
I am feeling lost inside without my ladylove
Because all flights are cancelled for me to get home
And all I have been waiting for is to hold my baby tight
After this long business trip being away for 6 months
I made plans to arrive home early while she's at work
As I called in a favor to a good friend since we were kids
And had a surprise ceremonial dinner reserved for two
At his restaurant to make up for our lost time being apart
And he planned to close down his place for the night just for us
But this storm is keeping me from getting home to my boo

As I try to call my ladylove on the phone all service is down
And now I am sitting here worrying about getting to her
Because my friend is going to lose out on money to help me
And I know I will owe him big time for his generosity
To make this a special coming home for me and my ladylove
And I cannot imagine the look on her face right now
Because she has been waiting for this day to come
Just as I walked to board the plane to come on this trip
She looked at me with tears building up in her eyes
And I began to miss her as I got closer and closer to my gate
Knowing that I was going to be gone for months from my boo

Now the storm seems to be getting heavier and heavier
As I just put my head in my hands and began to cry inside
I say a prayer to God and ask for him to ease up this storm
And not even five minutes goes by and the rain begins to stop
I looked out the window to see an amazing site outside
A colorful rainbow one of God's wonderful creations
And at the same time my phone rings and it's my baby

Telling me she sees on the news that my flight is cancelled
As I could hear the sadness and disappointment in her voice
Because she wanted me home more than anything in this world
And I told her don't worry I will be home soon in her arms
Right at that moment she dropped the phone and began to cry
My heart fell to the floor knowing that she was in pain
And I couldn't do anything to comfort and soothe my boo

All I can do right now is to call out her name over and over
Just so she would pick up the phone to hear my voice
And maybe it will calm her down for just a minute
So, I can ease her sorrow that is running through her veins
Because I have never heard her in this frame of mind before
And when she finally picked up the phone again
I took a deep breath to calm my nervous tension inside
And reassured my baby that everything will be ok
As soon as they give the thumbs up I will be on my way
To hold her in my arms and never ever let her go
Because my heart is breaking for my boo

I hear the splintering in her voice as she tries to talk to me
And at that very moment she says she has to hang up
At that very second I knew she was falling apart within
I try to call her back but she doesn't answer the phone
And now I am losing all control of my emotions
Because now my anxiety is working overtime on my psyche
Just not knowing what is running through my baby's mind
And with her not taking my calls I am becoming hysterical
As I need to get home as soon as possible to my boo

As I pace back and forth just waiting to board the plane
A cute older couple sees the distress on my face
And the elderly lady comes over and takes my hand
As she smiles at me and says everything will be fine

Because she sees that I am struggling with waiting
As she begins to say a prayer while holding my hand
And then proceeds to give me a hug and pats my back
Because she tells me that God loves me all the time
And he will see me through to get home to my love
Because she has faced what my baby is going through
As her husband walks up and says hang in their young man
And their kind words and actions helped ease my pain for my boo

Over the PA system we were called to board the plane
As I tried my ladylove one more time before we strapped in
And I still got no answer putting me back into panic mode
But sitting right across from me was that precious couple
He leaned over and said breathe son and don't worry
Because think about when you see your ladylove again
You will latch onto her and won't let her go until the end of time
Because son before I retired my wife and I shared your pain
But at the end of the day it makes moments like this worth it
Just imagine the flawless look on her face when she sees you
Because that moment will change your lives forever
Just to see the happiness and tears of my boo

As I sit back in my seat and close my eyes for the trip
And I drift off to sleep with her smile on my mind
Thinking of all the priceless times we shared together
Because each and every second summarized our lives
And there was no better feeling to experience with my love
As the turbulence caused me to awaken from my sleep
Making me slip back into a depressed state of mind
Because not knowing how my ladylove is coping
Is eating at the inner core deep within my soul
Because I am really concerned and missing my boo

My mind keeps wondering about how my baby is doing

As I look over at the couple and watch them closely
Because he slowly leans into her and gives her a kiss
And she shivers her body like it made her melt inside
At that same moment, you see her cheeks turn red
Like if it was her first kiss on their first date
As I sat back into my seat my heart began to tear
Because moments like that makes me miss my boo
As we hear from the captain to prepare for landing
My heart is beating a thousand miles a minute
And my palms are sweating as my hands begin to shake
Just knowing I will get to check on my heart and soul
Because she has been a nervous wreck worrying inside
And not being able to talk to her has ruined my spirit
Because she just won't answer my calls to calm my nerves
I know this is all due to me being away for so long
And when I finally get home I will make it up to her
As I will hold her tight and never let go of my boo

Now that we have landed and are off loading the plane
All I can anticipate is to get to the love of my life
And ease all her pain and anxiety from me not being home
But she has always been good about my travels for work
However, I never had seen her this unresponsive before
Because she has been my rock, my heartbeat and my backbone
And this business trip has caused her to fall to pieces
As she showed no signs of depression until the storm
That kept me from getting home to her on time
And she has always been a very strong woman
Because she would wrestle lions, tigers and bears
Just to stand tall and conquer all obstacles in life
and that is why she's my hero and my boo

I say goodbye to the amazing couple that held me together
And I received the biggest hug from them both

As they smiled and said hurry home to your love
Just promise us that you will spoil her rotten
And never ever stop telling her that you love her
Because in 40 years you both will be like us in life
And that miracle only happens to those that work hard
Because as we can see she always has your back
As they wave bye and walk away hand-in-hand
I just can't control my tears from falling down my face
Because I pray that I can experience moments like that
And grow old and grey for years with my boo

I hail a cab and begin to head home to my baby
And all I can think about is what is going on with her
Because she has not been like herself at all here lately
As I sit back and probe my brain on what might be wrong
All I can think of is she can't cope with my job
Because being gone months and months at a time
Has finally broke her spirit and damaged her soul
And the thought of this being the case is devastating me
Because my job comes second to my baby without a doubt
And no job will ever take her place as my number one
Because my world orbits around my best friend, my love, my boo

As I'm a block away from being in the arms of the one I adore
And I feel like a kid going to pick up my girl on a first date
Because I can't wait to lift her up and squeeze her tight
And spin her around and around until we get dizzy
As I kiss her uncontrollably until our lips get sore
Because nothing right now delights me more than her
And if I need to make up for this trip until the end of time
I will move heaven and earth to make this a reality
Not because I'm sorry but because she deserves the world
And that is what I feel deep inside my soul for my boo

I pay the cabbie and toss the bags on the porch and rush inside
As I shout for my love at the top of my lungs that I'm home
All I hear is a loud echo of my voice ringing throughout the house
And the silence in the house as I walk through is alarming
Because her car is in the driveway but she's not home
And I begin to worry knowing she seemed depressed today
So, I rush over to the neighbor's house which is her best friend
As I run up to the door she said she tried to call my phone
To let me know my baby got rushed to the hospital in pain
And at that very moment I drop to my knees in tears
Because my whole world feels like it is falling apart
As she helps me up to get me to the hospital in a hurry
And at this very moment my heart is heavy for my boo

When we pulled up to the hospital I jump out of the car
As I run up to the front desk and ask to see my ladylove
The nurse escorts me back to see her in the room
And before I enter the nurse says she may be out of it
But all I want to do is be by my ladylove's bedside
And the nurse walks me into the room to see my love
As she proceeds to tell me she is stable and doing good
And I ask what is going on with the queen of my kingdom
Because the nurse said my love wanted to tell me herself
And I said ok I will sit here and wait for her to wake up
As I pulled up the chair to hold her hand and pray to God
Because my soul is crying at the core for my boo

As the screech of the door startles me out of my sleep
And standing there in the light is my love's mother
With the look of concern and fear on her face
As her eyes are filling up with loads of tears
I jump up out of my seat to see what's wrong with her
As she tiptoes toward me to give me a great big hug
At that very moment, my heart begins to die inside

And for the first time in my entire life I am truly scared
Because I don't know what's wrong with my boo

I never prepared for anything like this to happen to us
As her mom held me tight while crying in my arms
And at that very moment I knew the news was serious
Because our lives were about to change forever
And at that very moment I heard my ladylove's soft voice
As I rushed over to lean down and cry on her chest in agony
She whispered I love you baby and I always will
And right then I lost all strength in my legs to stand
Because whatever was going on was not good for my boo

Her mother helped me to my feet as the doctor walked in
All I could see is the worry on his face as he cleared his throat
As soon as the doctor got close my ladylove said not yet doc
I want my baby to her this news from me with all present
She reached out and placed her hand inside of my hand
And for a split-second I felt my soul leave my body
As she told me she felt dizzy and collapsed in the house earlier
And the neighbors happened to find her laying at the front door
But she said that is not the worse of the news to swallow
At that very moment, her mom and the doctor moved next to me
As she took a deep breath and told me the earth-shattering news
That her test came back showing she has stage 4 cancer
And it has begun to rapidly spread throughout her body
It took all of the doctor's power and her mom to hold me up
As I look into the dying eyes of my world, my soulmate, my boo

My boo said don't cry because we made a lifetime of memories
And to take those memories and let them flow within my soul
Because God will watch over me in heaven and you on earth
As he will allow me to stop in to see you from time to time
And to touch your heart to keep you safe until we meet again

Just so you know my love you have always held me together
Through the darkest storms and conquered the highest mountains
And knowing how you never let me suffer through it alone
Makes my life's end game that much more magical for me
And I will cherish our love for eternity being your boo

After all of those breathtaking words from my ladylove
I leaned in and gave her a big hug and a long kiss
As I lifted up to look at her smile and beautiful eyes
Not knowing that my boo would take her last breath
I just lost everything in this world that I ever loved
As her mom said a prayer over her daughter's body
With her arms wrapped tight around my waist
As I looked upon my precious ladylove for the last time
Because my eternity just vanished out of my life, my boo

No One Else

The look in your eyes shows suffering
Because I made you cry tears of pain
By breaking the love & trust, we used to share
As I stare at you from across the room
I see the love of my life fading away
All I can think about is having you back
However, things are miles apart right now
All I want is to make it right for us
And you have made me feel love like no other
Because you have my heart in restraints
And nothing more in life matters to me
Because I can love no one else

Losing you felt like my life was going extinct
As a year went by without you, it hurt
Because I realized my world was in my hands
And I chose to shatter our happiness
Without thinking and killing the special love
We shared with each other in a blink of an eye
Just so you know I still want you always
Please let me know what it is for me to do
To have you once again to complete my future
Because I can love no one else

Your love was like the finest of all wines
As it cast a force field around my soul
And even with that ray of gold in my life
I hurt you deeply and I am deeply sorry
And I will give up everything to have you again
Because I have been lonely without you
All I want is a second chance to prove my worth
That you were my world and I let you down
Because I want no one else

If I have to beg then that is what I will do
Because I am struggling without you
As it is causing me sleepless nights
With you on my mind and in my dreams
Because I will do anything to have you
If you give us another try to be one again
And this time, I promise to never let you go
Because you are the pinnacle of my life
And I want no one else

Perfect Crush

My feelings grow deep within my heart for you
And my soul lights up like the sun in love
Because the time we spend together is like a fairytale
That has turned into a dream that has come true
I cannot provide you with diamonds and pearls
With the house you daydreamed about as a little girl
But I will love you forever until my very last breath
And will do my best to make you happy day by day
No matter how much my mind thinks the worse
Because I now believe this is not a fantasy
As when you touch me I feel the love in your heart
Because it is like a rainbow hovering over my soul
And the love you have for me is like a pot of gold
That keeps me going through life's challenges
And that love you share with me is spine-tingling
As it permits my soul to fall deep in love with you
Because I Love you and you're my Perfect Crush

Precious Angel

It has been 5 years since I have been home
And I know that my mom will be excited
However, I cannot wait to see her smile
And how hard it must have been on her
Because of the falling out we had
And the harsh words we said to each other
But I have committed to making things right
Because I cannot see myself without my mom
And if something were to happen to her
I would not be able to forgive myself
Because she is my precious angel

I am on my way home to see my mom
And I get butterflies just like when I was little
However, I know once I can hug her
And squeeze her tight they will go away
Because she always made me feel safe
Nevertheless, it is going to be a big surprise to her
Because she does not know I am on my way
As I close my eyes for a few minutes to catch some Z's
I begin to dream of my childhood with my mom
She had always had my best intentions at heart
Because she was always playing the dual parent role
And it drove me crazy because she was so strict
Nevertheless, everything she did made me a better man
Because she is my precious angel

I love my mom more and more today than ever before
Because as I look back on my life she gave me shelter
As she allowed me to grow as an individual
And it was a hard thing to swallow as a young boy

But even tougher as I became a young teen
Because I thought she was the worst parent in the world
However, she had her reason behind all of her actions
Because it made me realize as I grew into a man

What she did for me was a blessing in disguise
However, it took me until adulthood to understand her madness
And she did it all out of love for me as her child
Because if you would have told me then what I know now
That I made it this far with her rules in my life
Looking back on these memories I would do it all over again
And I wouldn't trade her in for anything in this world
Because she is my precious angel

As the hour rolls on by and I begin to awake from my nap
I hear the train conductor call out my upcoming stop
And I am getting excited to get off to head home
To my dear mom to hold her in my arms once again
It will make me feel as if I am that runny-nose kid
That she used to sing to at night if I could not sleep
And put Vick's on my chest if I had a major cold
Because she made me feel like no other kid in this world
However, sometimes we take things for granted in life
And I know I did and that was the woman I call mom
Because she was so uncompromising with everything
Nevertheless, it was for my own personal quality of life
As I think of those memories, I begin to cry
Because she is my precious angel

As the tears flow from my eyes and down my face
Because of all these recollections comes moments of joy
And they will stick with me until my dying day
Because she gave me more happiness than I could imagine
And I just want to make things right between us

To feel the warmth that she provided me
Just like I was growing up when I was small
Because no matter what she will be my one & only mom
And I want to cherish that for an eternity
Even if it means sacrificing my own pride
And become the caring person she raised me to be
Because she is my precious angel

As the cab pulls up in front of her house, I open the door
And I reach in my pocket to pay the cabbie his fare
I hear the little voices of the neighborhood kids playing
As I look over to see them playing tag through the yard
And I had an instant flashback of me running around
Because those were some of the greatest times in my life
I begin to smile as I approach the front door
My nerves begin to jump out of control inside
Just as I ring the doorbell and wait for her to answer
And I hear the creaking of the door slowly opening
As I look at the emotion on her face of joy & pain
I drop my bags and hold open my arms to give her a hug
And the shock makes her almost faint in my arms
Because now I can hold my precious angel

As we hold each other tight watching our tears flow
I cannot even get my words out because of the joy I feel
However, I know that this was long overdue for us
Because we vowed to never speak to one another ever again
And I knew that if something happened to my mom
I would never have been able to forgive myself inside
And it would have haunted my soul eternally forever
However, I refused to let that happen to my mom and me
Because she means the world to me without a doubt
And this moment is just another special memory for us
As we just cling to one another for what seems like a lifetime

Because I know she has missed me oh so much
As I tell her I am sorry for my unkind words I said to her
Because I would never ever in my life hurt her intentionally
And she just told me it was all right and she has forgiven me
As I dropped to my knees and prayed to God
She wrapped her arms around me tight
And it made me feel so good from head to toe
Because I have been forgiven by my precious angel

Pretty Smile

I had thoughts of never being happy
Then all of a sudden along came you
Standing at 5' 4" with luscious skin
And silky dark brown hair
With eyes that change in the light
And a body that drives men wild
However, what I noticed the most about you
Was that heart melting pretty smile

As my anticipation of meeting you
Was having me blush all over
Then the time was nearing for us to meet
As you pulled up and got off your bike
I could not wait to see you up close
Then all I could say was oh Wow
Because you were more beautiful
Than your pictures showcased
And then when you introduced yourself
My heart started to skip a beat
I felt my entire body begin to shiver
However, what I noticed the most about you
Was that heart melting pretty smile

I feel like you are in another league
Because you are prettier than all get out
It was incredible to me that you think I am cute
Nevertheless, I still cannot get over your smile
Because it is the most glamorous thing I have ever seen
As it can hypnotize the mighty king of the jungle
If I was in the jungle, you can make me roar
Because it has penetrated into my soul
My eyes cannot stop staring at you continuously
Because it makes you blush as I stare at you
You cannot help but to imagine what is on my mind
Because the look I have told my story about you
All you can do is shake your head and smile
As you stand in front of me glowing
With that heartwarming pretty smile

Spirit Adrift

You are a blast from my past lifetime
It was great seeing your face again
Because it made feelings rise to the surface
As I had locked those feelings for you away
It felt unreal to feel this way for you again
And the funny thing is we never were a couple
That is the shocking thing with fantasy & dreams
Because my heart was with someone else
Nevertheless, your beauty had my spirit adrift

never knew how you felt about me until just now
Because we spoke to one another through email
A light began to shine bright with every key stroke
That we had more in common than we realized
Because you found out, I was single and free
And your interest was piqued along with your feelings
Because you are in a relationship going nowhere
Without all of the things that you want and need
And it has you mentally lost and confused
Because he has your spirit adrift

This whole thing of us has major ramifications
However, I am willing to take the risk on you
Because I always imagined us as a couple
You held a spell on my mind, body and soul
I always had the enticing urge to kiss you
Because your juicy lips made my muscles twitch
As I stared and watched your every motion
What I felt watching you walk past was oh so sweet
Because it left my spirit adrift

Now that we both feel the same, what comes next?
Should we see what fate has in store for us?
Do we just go our separate ways and move on?
Without finding out what has brought us together
Or just allow our hearts to crumble to dust
Because we never took the chance on each other
As we go on in life asking ourselves what if
Never knowing and allowing our souls to become one
As our hearts begin to sail in different ways
While our blood pressures carry our spirit adrift

Sweet Gentle Woman

Life has its bumps in the road with twists and turns
However, the first time I met you was amazing
I felt like a kid in a candy store as my eyes lit up
Seeing your pictures did not capture your true beauty
Because what was standing in front of me was so amazing
Your exquisite beauty caused my body to be hot and steamy
As I tried to avoid looking into your sexy eyes
It made my heart jump out of my chest and melt in your hands
As I braced myself from staggering before I fell down
Your smile captivated the entire room as everyone stared
All I could do to maintain myself was to say WOW!
Because I finally met a sweet gentle woman

We talked for hours as the rain came down outside
With the softness of your voice that mesmerizes my soul
As I felt short of breath as I gasped for air
Because you brought a source of pleasure into my body
As an authentic passion oozed out of my pores
In all my years of existence I have never felt this way
Because you added passion, love and faith to my life
I thank God for you every night before I go to sleep
Because I finally met a sweet gentle woman

My dreams of you would wake me from a deep sleep
I could not believe you choose me out of many
Because with your beauty you could have anyone
And when our eyes connected it was like paradise
Because I could read your thoughts inside your soul
And those thoughts were pure, sweet and genuine
As my head spun like a tornado with you on my mind
While my heart went pity pat like never before
Because I knew heaven brought me a sweet gentle woman

To Love and To Hold

My mind is working overtime
Because all I can do is think of you
My mind keeps playing tricks on my heart
As the hours pass on by slowly
Just knowing I cannot wait for that moment
To be with my baby again
Even though we have differences with each other
I just need to be home to make things right
Because all I do is think of you
As my life feels empty without you
I cannot sleep, eat or think straight
Just knowing that you could be gone
I hope and pray that we can work it out
Because I need you in my life
To love and to hold

As I catch a uber to the airport to head home to my baby
I keep having flashbacks of our times together
Looking back upon the good and the bad times
And the last sad moment we shared before my trip
I just hope that you still love me
Because I cannot imagine you not in my life
Because with you gone I would fall apart inside
While things have not been the same in my life
Because you were my driving force to survive
And to lose you would just stop my heart from beating
To love and to hold

As my flight touches down on the runway
I begin to get chills up and down my spine
Because I am praying you give me a second chance
As I can't wait to hold you close in my arms
Because you are the love that blossomed in my life
And I want everything we once shared again
Because your love is the medicine to my soul
And your sweet kisses I long for minute by minute
As my heart embraces for your soothing touch
To love and to hold

Vibrant Angel

Often I take things in life for granted
And as I think of you I'm totally supplanted
From all of the things great and small
That you have done for me makes you stand tall
With the love and sacrifices you gave me
And God helped you mold me
Every day I see your smile it humbles me
And the joy you bring to my heart & soul blesses me
Because you're my Vibrant Angel

I want to pass on to my kids your great blessings
Because I know that as I grew you kept me guessing
And even though I hated your rules
It made me blossom into this wonderful jewel
As the years continue to pass you by
My heart and eyes thinking of you lights the sky
And I know you have given me your all
For me to be the best in life and stand tall
Because what I've learned from you makes me shine
As I share my thoughts with family and this glass of wine
And so you know you make everything in my life fine
Because you're my Vibrant Angel

WOW!

Night falls out here sitting around the campfire
Just picturing what life would be like without you
Because when I first laid eyes on you, I caught a case
As I fell head over heels with infatuation for you
Because I loved the way you walked, talked and smiled
I even loved the sweet scent of your perfume
That left a trail of men walking around in a daze
Because not even the beast within me could resist
However, I knew from that day I had to have you
Because I could not get my head out of the clouds
And the only thing I could mumble under my breath is WOW!

While the stars shined bright in the midnight sky
As my heart weakens every time I think of you
And my nerves have never been jumpy before in my life
But when you're around, it all makes sense to me
Because you make my whole world spin out of control
And all I can do is avoid being around you
Because I cannot let you see me this way ever again
As you already whisper things to your friends
Laughing and giggling when I'm around
But all I can picture in my mind is WOW!

As I haven't slept all night as the sun comes up
And man, oh man how breathtaking you are to me
Because the thought of you set my soul on fire
Which kept me up all night simmering hot inside
And all the different images of you mesmerizes my mind
As my feelings run through my body like a heard of buffalo
Because I can't escape the hold you have on me
As each passing moment, you make my heart say WOW!

www.ingramcontent.com/pod-product-compliance
Lightning Source LLC
LaVergne TN
LVHW041810060526
838201LV00046B/1206